a New Look for Sunday Morning

a New Look for Sunday Morning

William Beaven Abernethy

Nashville ABINGDON New York

A NEW LOOK FOR SUNDAY MORNING

Library of Congress Cataloging in Publication Data

Abernethy, William B 1939-
A new look for Sunday morning.
Includes bibliographical references. 1. South Congregational Church, Middletown, Conn. 2. Public worship—Case studies. 3. Religious education—Case studies. I. Title.
BX7255.M63S682 264'.05'8 74-34387

ISBN 0-687-27805-8

MANUFACTURED BY THE PARTHENON PRESS AT
NASHVILLE, TENNESSEE, UNITED STATES OF AMERICA

Contents

Foreword 9

Chapter 1 One Service in Three Acts 15
South Church at a Glance 22
From Eleven to Ten O'Clock 24
The Experimental Church School 26
A Separate Church and Church School 28
Two Kinds of Worship 31
1971—An Open-Ended Evaluation 32
A New Sunday Morning Program 34
A Theology or Rationale for the New Program 35
Practical Refinements 37
A Beginning 40
A Christmas Pageant 41
Questions for the Future 44

Chapter 2 Worship 47
Historical Worship Patterns 49
Modern Criticisms of Formal and Informal Worship 52
Formal and Informal Worship: A Both-And 54
The Effect of Celebration on Worship 55

A Youth Sunday 56
Traditional Worship in Act One 60
The Tradition: Remembering and Responding 61
A Covenant Renewal Ceremony 63
Education and Traditional Worship 65
Formal Worship 67
Content in Formal Worship 69
Formal Rituals 70
Family Worship—Pluralistic Age Levels 71
Children in Act One 73
Why Family Worship? 75
Summary 76

Chapter 3 Education 78
Examples of the Teaching of Religion 81
Education After Worship 83
Education Before Celebration 85
The Effect on Education of Being In-Between 87
The Content of Act Two 90
Courses on Religious Topics 93
Courses Focusing on Personal Relationships 94
Involving People in the Process of Learning 96
The December Family Project 98
Planning for the Education Program 101
Putting Act Two Together 103
Coffee and Juice 105
Act Two Leads into Celebration 107

Chapter 4 Celebration 109
Celebration as Congregational Worship 111
Celebration as Play 114
Celebration as Outreach 117
The Content of Celebration 119
1. Fellowship 119
2. Healing 121
3. Religious Festivals 122

4. Acting Out Biblical Stories 123
5. Important Church Events 125
6. Coordination with Education Courses 126
7. Development of Celebration Rituals 127
8. Allowing Room for Spontaneity 127
9. Reacting to Important Events in the World 128
10. Celebrating in Different Places 130
11. Seasons of the Year 131
12. Important Personal Events 131
The Model Order for Celebration 132
A Balance of Planning and Spontaneity 135
Celebration as the Participation of Amateurs 138

Chapter 5 Communion Background 141
Discerning Christ's Presence 143
Communion as Standard 146
Communion and the Three-Part Program 147
The Idea of Sacrament 148
Communion, Consecration, and Sacrament 149
The Interaction of Communion and Celebration 152
Biblical Sacrifices and Offerings 155
General Biblical Consecrations 160
Children, Celebration, and Communion 162
A Final Word: The Risk of Presumption 167

Epilogue 169
Notes 175

Foreword

A woman called some time ago to ask whether a group from her church might be able to visit on a Sunday morning to see what our church was doing.

"Sure," I replied.

She went on to explain that their Sunday school was in trouble. Children were losing interest and not coming. Teachers were hard to find. She had heard about the South Congregational Church of Middletown and wanted to come up and see whether we could give them ideas to "jazz up" their church school.

I hesitated. It was easy to sympathize with their problem. What parish has not faced that same problem to some extent? Our particular efforts at South Church to develop something new date back in part to similar difficulties. But these efforts have not been directed towards "jazzing up" a Sunday school. Instead, we have tried to bring new depth and vitality to the congregation as a whole by integrating our worship life and religious education program within one two-hour service on Sunday morning. Her group was still welcome to come, of course, and we did have ideas to share about religious education. But they might want to know our goals beforehand so as to know what to expect in a visit.

"Oh," she responded, "we're not concerned about worship. We like our minister."

That stopped me for a minute. I had hoped that concern for worship and affection for the worship leader were not mutually exclusive! Eventually, as I remember it, her group did come for a visit and did gather some new ideas. I was disappointed, however, by the arbitrary limits she seemed to be placing on the search to revitalize church education.

Too often a congregation's life is compartmentalized. Worship is what adults do in the sanctuary on Sunday morning, usually at eleven o'clock. Religious education is something different, a program for children which takes place outside the sanctuary in the other rooms of the church building. Church and church school customarily exist as relatively separate and unrelated institutions. What we miss is the deepened faith and creativity which can be released within all ages of the church membership when these parallel institutions are brought together in a process of dynamic interaction and cross-fertilization.

This book was written out of the history, the dreams, and the practical experience of one particular parish in trying to integrate church and church school. Our effort centers around the development of a three-part Sunday morning program of worship, education, and celebration. A full, but condensed, conventional church service is followed by Sunday school offerings for all ages; the morning is tied together at the end by a time of celebration, a period of informal, spontaneous, spirited worship. The total two-hour service is, in effect, one drama in three acts.

There is special value in writing out of the day-to-day struggles and rewards, frustrations and successes, of people who are actually engaged in the process of developing new patterns of church life. We will not be giving a diagnosis of what appears to be wrong with the church and then calling on someone else to prescribe the cure. Nor is this simply a book of theory. What follows is the story and the implications of one program which tries to integrate worship, education, and celebration from the perspective of persons who are actually doing it.

Obviously, there are risks, too, in writing out of the experience of a particular situation. At the head of the list is the risk of seeming to imply that South Church is the model of the way things ought to be. Such an implication would be false. This Middletown congregation is far from perfect, full of human beings with all the weaknesses and strengths which any group of persons might be expected to have.

In addition, every congregation, of whatever denomination, has its own distinctive history, membership, needs, and hopes. What makes sense in one parish at one time in history will not necessarily make sense in exactly the same way to another with different theological emphases, size, composition, and budget. It is wisest to acknowledge at the outset that probably no one definitive model for parish life exists.

Again, it would be a mistake to claim that South Church's two-hour Sunday morning program of worship, education, and celebration has proved to be the definitive answer for all the hopes and needs of this particular congregation. A fairer statement would recognize that the two-hour service has met some problems and raised some new problems, shifting the frontier of our concern.

Despite the risk of pretentiousness, however, we do believe there has been value in this shifting of frontiers in our parish's concerns. It is as though worship, education, and celebration produce a far richer sound when they are played in harmony than when they are played alone. It is the richer sound and the harmony that we wish to share with others. You may need to transpose the key or change the particular instruments or vary the rhythm or change the size of the orchestra to fit your situation. But we trust that the harmony you can find in your own way will amply reward the effort in trying to integrate these areas of church life.

This is not a one-sided book of practice alone or of theory alone. Practical factors are immensely important, and we will examine them. How did the congregation get to the point of deciding to integrate worship, education, and celebration? What happened? Has there been a backlash? How do you work it out week by week? Who does the planning? How does the three-part program wear over a period of months, or years? If some of these questions can be answered through the life of one parish, other persons might be encouraged to ask the same questions and answer these questions in their own way.

There is a danger, though, in a one-sided book of practical suggestions alone. A how-to-do-it manual without any integrating vision to help organize the suggestions can lead to a haphazard attempt to try anything which looks different and promising, with no understanding of the essence of what one is trying to do and why.

What follows is an effort to balance the discussion of practical experience with a discussion of the theory behind it. The assumption here is that theology—an understanding of how God acts in human history—can be hammered out on the forge of practical parish life. I hope that the discussion of theory along with the discussion of practice may help in the process of translating what is of value from one church's experience to other communities of faith. Theory and practice together may be able to move us beyond an all too easy response to a book of this kind: a "Wouldn't it be nice" coupled with an "Of course it would never work" and an "Even if it could work we could never try it here."

I want to express special thanks here to Ann, my wife, whose spirit and personal ministry to and with the whole congregation, including its minister, have been of immeasurable value in helping to bring us through the trials of a period of creativity in the church to a time of renewed hope for a warm, open, and supportive community of faith.

Mary Klaaren, first as a lay leader in the parish and then as a staff member with Christian education responsibilities, has been outstanding both in the dreaming of new dreams for Sunday morning church life and in the challenge of translating these dreams into reality. Milo Wilcox, who served as the highest elected lay officer in the church for over three years of the experience described in this book, deserves major credit for setting a tone in which this congregation could take a realistic and significant leap of faith. And Madlyn Combe has been of particular help in her sensitive reading, and working with, the manuscript of this book during its preparation.

Let me affirm finally that in the most fundamental way this book has been written by all the members of South Church, whose commitment, whose willingness to risk, and whose participation and shared leadership throughout an exciting and difficult venture, have made a book possible. The "we" used throughout this book is honest and grateful testimony to the continuing truth of that sentence in the church covenant: "We believe that lay members of the church and the minister share the responsibility of serving in Christ's mission."

The pages ahead are an attempt to share a corporate vision, a sense of excitement and a feeling of adventure about "a new look for Sunday morning" which have led one congregation of people to hope that others may be stimulated to work out variations on a theme. The more we have lived with the scope and complexity which is involved in trying to integrate worship, education, and celebration, the more we have come to realize our need to learn from the experience and the criticism of others. There are, we know, differing perspectives, new insights, and creative new possibilities which we cannot hope to find within the necessarily confining limitations of the imagination and energy of relatively few people. We share with others in the hope of learning from others.

1
One Service in Three Acts

People came to worship that Sunday at their usual time of ten o'clock. The service was relatively conventional Protestant worship: scripture and sermon, music and prayer, and an offering. The congregation sat in rows of pews to be led in their worship by the minister at the front and the choir and organist in the balcony at the rear of the sanctuary.

The service was built around the twenty-first chapter of Jeremiah. The prophet was speaking to the people of the Old Testament nation of Judah some twenty-five hundred years ago at a time when that nation was under attack by the powerful armies of Babylonia. Judah's very existence as an independent nation was threatened. Yet Jeremiah did not speak words of comfort but a harsh warning: "Thus says the Lord, the God of Israel: Behold, I will turn back the weapons of war which are in your hands. . . . I myself will fight against you with outstretched hand and strong arm" (vv. 4-5).

Jeremiah's message was not easy to hear at the time he gave it. His words are equally difficult for us to hear today. He talks of a God of love, but this love includes the stern note of judgment against a people when they are wrong. National security, for Jeremiah, is to be found in national repentance for sin and not in the accumulation of military hardware. He adds the warning that God may use against us the very weapons we build for our protection if we reject his laws.

The sermon that morning talked about the war in Vietnam. The end of that war was not as yet in sight. American soldiers were still fighting in that increasingly unpopular conflict. The minister wondered whether Jeremiah's words were not relevant to the involvement of the United States in that war. Could not God's love for America be speaking a word of judgment against us at a time when we were in the wrong? Could not God be calling us to national repentance for our policies in Southeast Asia?

Not everyone in the congregation agreed with that sermon. Some had served in the armed forces in Vietnam—or had sons or other relatives there—and these persons brought the light of intense personal experience to bear on their agreement or disagreement with the message from the pulpit.

Conventional Protestant worship, however, does not provide the best opportunity for argument or discussion. The listeners that morning had little chance during the opening service to respond, debate, challenge, affirm what they had heard. There was opportunity for prayer and meditation, for the singing of hymns related to God's concern for peace, but many in the congregation were still stirred up at the singing of the final hymn. A controversial sermon stimulated the congregation and left people with unfinished business at the end of worship.

The service was only about forty-five minutes long. It was followed immediately by an education program open to all ages with a variety of different courses offered for various groups of people throughout the church building. One of the courses attracted a large group who stayed that particular Sunday in the sanctuary for the showing of a slide presentation on the war in Southeast Asia. Pictures of highly advanced computerized technology were followed by pictures of the results of that technology in human agony and suffering, in the devastation of land and property.

The audience in the class watched and listened to the slide presentation. It was hard not to be moved emotionally by what we were seeing and hearing, even the tables of facts and figures. When the slides were over, there was time for response and discussion. What people said was relatively familiar to a country which had been debating and arguing about Vietnam for a decade.

Some felt that the slide presentation was too one-sided, showing American weapons and technology with far greater emphasis than it did the weapons and technology of the enemy. One person questioned the accuracy of the tables of figures shown in the slides. Others spoke of the human agony we had seen so graphically depicted and wondered why the war need continue even a minute longer.

Someone touched on the relationship of the war to faith. What did the slide show have to do with religious education? Why show such pictures in a church sanctuary? Others felt that the scripture lesson from Jeremiah and the sermon during worship had given ample testimony to the Bible's concern for issues of war and peace, such as Vietnam. Another countered by wondering what relevance a story from twenty-five hundred years ago in biblical times could or should have on modern political and military policy in this country.

If the opening worship left many people stirred up at its conclusion, this education class did little to settle people's questions. It may well be that the arguments over Southeast Asia cannot be decided with any degree of consensus until history gives us the perspective of a generation or so on that conflict. Yet the class did give people a chance to become personally involved, to share their feelings and ideas, to speak and to have other people listen. By the end of that education class, the discussion about the war had moved from being essentially a monologue by the minister during the sermon to becoming a heated discussion within a particular group of highly involved participants.

At about twenty minutes to twelve, all the courses came to an end, and people throughout the church building came back to the sanctuary for what we call the celebration period. Children of ages three to five came down from the parish house to join the rest of the church in this final time of spontaneous worship. The congregation came to try to tie the loose ends of the morning together, to regather as a community of faith before each one of us went his or her separate way into the world outside.

Yet, what possible meaning could celebration have on that Sunday? What could we do together in an open-ended, twenty-minute period of time whose purpose was to celebrate the living presence of God in our midst? Those who had seen the slide show were either numb from its devastating impact or caught up in a mood ready for a knock-down-drag-out argument. Others from different classes with a variety of topics of concern had moved somewhat beyond the issue of Vietnam which had been laid out in the morning's sermon.

The congregation gathered at the front of the sanctuary, closer together physically than we had been during ten o'clock worship. Some sat in the front pews. Others sat on the steps of the chancel. A few simply stood close enough to the center of the group of people for us to hear each other under the high ceiling of a Gothic sanctuary. Small children moved freely about, but most people were not upset by the movement; somehow it seemed appropriate to the informality of the mood.

The minister called people together at the beginning of the celebration service and admitted that it was particularly difficult that Sunday to know what we might do to celebrate the experiences of war and destruction we had shared that morning. He reminded the people, however, that we were gathered to celebrate the presence of God in Christ. This goal could mean celebrating the broken body of the suffering Christ as well as celebrating the new life of the Risen Christ. The congregation settled down into relative silence, groping its way into a time which was unplanned and an experience which was unknown.

Quietly one person started to talk about the mood he felt in people that morning, struggling with the rightness or wrongness, the pain and the suffering, of a war that kept coming back to haunt each of us, regardless of what we felt about it. The mood seemed to reflect shock or sadness, anger or guilt, but each person was trying to cope with something that was bigger than all of us together. Another commented that it wasn't really appropriate to argue in a worship service. As we moved together slowly into an atmosphere of worship, we seemed to agree by our silence. The intense need to argue melted away.

How could we consecrate the morning with all its emotion, its unanswered questions, its terrible impact? One woman came up with the idea that we sing the spiritual "Kum Ba Yah," but that we change the words. She suggested that we sing, "Someone's burning, Lord," and, "Someone's dying, Lord." Someone had brought a guitar and he took it up to play it. The organist moved to a piano we had at the front of the sanctuary.

That was probably the most difficult song many of us had sung in a long time. We couldn't look each other in the eye. Several persons broke down and wept, especially when we went on singing to add the traditional verses of that spiritual and came to "Someone's crying, Lord." Many got down on their knees to sing, "Someone's praying, Lord." We concluded with "Someone's singing, Lord" as the volume grew and people gradually lifted up their heads to look at each other and manage a smile out of the tears.

Glancing around that congregation, one could see the Vietnam veteran who was still struggling with memories of his service there and with the pain of trying to integrate those memories into his family life at home. There were parents of soldiers still in Southeast Asia, who lived with the fear that something might happen to them. Two of those present were the parents of conscientious objectors who had asked for and received the spiritual support of the church's Board of Deacons. One could see veterans of earlier wars who had done their service when it was their turn and felt that both they and the country had gained as a result. All were singing "Kum Ba Yah."

At the end of the song we found ourselves in a period of silence, unplanned yet powerful in its impact. There were still no answers. The arguments would go on with people in that congregation on both sides of almost every one of them. But we seemed to feel in that silence a presence which bound us together with a common experience of what it means to be human in a broken world. People dared to believe that we were gathered in the presence of Jeremiah's God, who loves us and judges us, whose judgment is an expression of his love.

When the silence had run its course, the minister led the congregation in the passing of the Peace of Christ. Individuals shared whatever words, handshakes, or gestures of caring they felt appropriate. The congregation then joined hands for the final benediction and the singing of the chorus of "Kum Ba Yah." At noon, the whole two-hour service of worship, education, and celebration was over, and the congregation left for home and Sunday dinner.

The above experience took place in the spring of 1972 at the South Congregational Church of Middletown, Connecticut. That parish had made the decision a few months earlier to adopt a two-hour service in three parts as its regular weekly Sunday morning program. The Vietnam Sunday illustration helps to illustrate the program and its intention of trying to integrate worship, education, and celebration in the life of the church.

The weekly pattern at South Church is relatively simple. We begin with a conventional Protestant worship service at ten o'clock, though the attempt is made to involve children as young as first-graders in at least a part of what is happening throughout. At 10:50 the congregation breaks up into small groups for education classes for all ages. Individuals may choose from a varied menu of courses depending on their interest, and classes may run for a month or longer depending on the particular content involved. Finally, every Sunday the congregation is called back to the sanctuary at 11:40 for a twenty-minute period of celebration, described in the weekly bulletin as "Open Worship—focusing on Spirit, personal involvement, congregational sharing in faith." Persons are encouraged to come for all or part of the two-hour service, depending on interest and desire.

A two-hour, three-part service is a new church form in many ways. We are not interested in newness for the sake of newness, however. Everything new is not automatically good, nor is everything old to be discarded. Much of what this book is all about is thoroughly familiar to persons who have lived and worked and struggled—and all too often agonized—to try to make their church conform to its biblical promise by keeping what is valid from the past while changing that which needs to be renewed.

We have also learned that many times something which appears new turns out to be a recovery of a practice that is quite old. A strong member of South Church who had struggled through the development of the three-part service along with everyone else—and on occasion expressed strong reservations about it—commented recently that what we were doing was not really that new. He remembered going to church during his childhood in another denomination and another part of the country. His memory was of a formal worship service followed by Sunday school for young and old, and of a brief closing worship time to pull things together before people went home.

Perhaps South Church has developed the three-part service in unique ways, but others have tried similar programs before. There is no desire in this account to spend time trying to demonstrate precisely how unique our congregation or its program actually is. We hope instead to support all those who already share the broader vision which has captured us and to encourage those whose vision is different to enter into dialogue with us so that we may both learn and grow.

In developing new patterns of church life one is struck again and again with the importance of traditional forms to church members. The church's past lives on in the customs and conventions of the present. Many persons have come to depend on the patterns of the past to support and shape their faith. Even those who reject traditional patterns may be dependent on those patterns in a way, as a focal point for rebellion. The point is that one may generate far more heated response by an attempt to change the order of worship, for example, than by a highly controversial sermon within the regular order.

Creating new forms of parish life, such as a new Sunday morning program, is not, then, simply a matter of artistic vision or administrative skill. The task requires pastoral sensitivity and compassion toward the particular people who make up that congregation. With this idea in mind let us look briefly at the nature of South Church as a particular congregation of people in order to see the background for a three-part Sunday morning program of worship, education, and celebration.

South Church at a Glance

The South Congregational Church is a congregation of between four and five hundred members with an annual overall budget of some fifty to sixty thousand dollars. Denominationally, it belongs to the United Church of Christ. The composition of the membership is reflected in the leadership of the parish. The executive committee of the church's governing board was composed recently of a regional planner, a doctor, a high school student, a computer expert, a homemaker, a hardware store salesman, and the minister. Boards and committees in the congregation may draw on business people, teachers, bankers, workers in industry, secretaries, insurance salesmen, nurses.

A strong and influential group of members is connected with Wesleyan University, including professors and administrators. A mailman, a farmer, a welfare recipient, a welfare worker, hospital laboratory technicians, a free-lance writer, the owner of a local business—all have worked in the organizational structure in one way or another. Most, though not all, of the members are white.

The church building stands at the south end of Main Street in Middletown, Connecticut, a city of some 37,000 inhabitants.

When the Reverend Ebenezer Frothingham founded the church 228 years ago out of the Great Awakening in American church history, he wanted to find a more "enthusiastic" church life than he felt was possible in the already established First Congregational Church at the center of town. Nowadays, First Church and South Church look out on a community with a strong Roman Catholic population, a variety of different Protestant denominations, several black churches, a Jewish synagogue, and some Pentecostal and fundamentalist sects.

In recent years South Church has attracted a number of imaginative and dedicated people—persons with a commitment to the basic content of traditional Christian faith, yet individuals who believe that traditional faith may need new forms of expression if many today are to know that faith with the vitality it deserves. The congregation also includes a number of families whose commitment to this parish goes back many, many years.

During the decade of the 1960s, South Church opened itself to the tensions and the polarizations of that period of turmoil in American history. The country was struggling with the Chicago Democratic Convention of 1968, the Vietnam War protests, Black Power, and the increasing breakdown of communication between liberals and conservatives. The winds and storms of change on Main Street blew inside this Middletown church as they did inside many another church sanctuary. The South Church is still wrestling today with what it means to be a responsible "downtown church" in a community of racial tensions and urban renewal, of strains between town and gown, of poor communication between various ethnic groups.

As the 1970s began, the congregation found itself torn and divided. Some parts of the social action undertaken within the church came to be highly controversial. People whose commitment to the church was deep found that commitment strained as they tried to hold on to others in the same congregation who seemed to be on the opposite side of issue after issue in the parish life. Our humanness showed through again and again. For many of us, the period was a time of pain and a time of suffering.

The combination of imaginative and dedicated people plus a time of intense polarization and suffering led us to both the possibility of innovation and the necessity of innovation. The science of chemistry may be helpful here. That science knows of reactions in which separate elements combine to form a new chemical compound when the heat becomes high enough. The heat at South Church became pretty high for a while. But out of suffering came something new, the integration of the separate elements of worship, education, and celebration to form a new compound of a single Sunday morning service in three acts.

Chemistry knows of compounds which are formed at high heat, which remain stable when that heat is reduced. Though it may take a high temperature to create the compound initially, if the new substance is stable it will remain in its new form at a variety of temperatures. It is our belief that the South Church program of integrating worship, education, and celebration is a stable compound even when the heat is reduced. The two-hour service continues to serve us well now that the mood of congregational controversy has receded.

Other parishes facing strains and tensions similar to those of this Middletown congregation may find a consideration of the three-part Sunday morning service to be of value in their particular search for reconciliation. Yet we have discovered parishes without such strains who have also found value in the three-part service on its own merits. Indeed, South Church itself is only beginning to see some of the exciting possibilities in that Sunday morning format—possibilities that may have been hidden from us by the particular history through which we came.

From Eleven to Ten O'Clock

For as far back as some long-time members could remember, South Church had gathered for worship on Sundays at the familiar eleven o'clock hour. The children came an hour or so earlier for Sunday school, and then some stayed to sit through the beginning of worship with their families. At one point during worship, these children would leave for what was called crafts class, an activity period for the remainder of the service time.

By the end of the 1960s, however, the crafts class had become a church headache. Fewer and fewer adults were willing to volunteer to organize and supervise what had become little more than a chaotic baby-sitting period of nonproductive busy-work. A variety of minor adjustments in the Sunday morning schedule was tried, but each adjustment brought its own particular set of new problems.

In February of 1969, the congregation made the crucial decision to change its hour of worship from eleven o'clock to ten. Children were still to worship with their families for the first part of the service as before, but the dreaded crafts class was now replaced by Sunday school, rescheduled to take place as soon as the children left the sanctuary.

It may be difficult for those who have not gone through the experience to imagine how traumatic it can be for a congregation to change its customary worship pattern of years and years. The underlying security of the familiar worship hour of eleven o'clock can be of immense importance. When South Church changed its time of service in 1969, many long-time members felt that "things weren't the way they used to be—and the way that they ought to continue to be." The sense of congregational turmoil already brewing through controversial social action was significantly increased.

The changed hour also led to a substantial decrease in church school attendance. Under the old pattern many parents who did not themselves wish to attend worship were able to bring their children to Sunday school at 9:30 and pick them up at 11:00. Obviously, these children did not stay through the first part of the church service at eleven, nor were they involved in crafts class.

The new format, however, stressed the expectation that children would begin their religious education by attending the first part of church with their parents. The expectation placed more pressure on parents to attend worship. Families who were already used to sitting through the first part of an eleven o'clock service together found it relatively easy to do the same at ten. But the adults who did not want to come to church themselves felt that it was harder to drop their children off at church for religious training. Many of the latter parents simply stopped bringing their children altogether.

Religious educators might well argue that such a decrease in church school attendance is not necessarily bad. How much value is there in a religious education program for children when the adult members of the family are not interested enough in religious faith to come to church themselves? Such a philosophical question does need to be answered. But regardless of the answer, the fact of decreased Sunday school attendance can be unsettling for a church. Once again there was reason for South Church turmoil.

The Experimental Church School

The change of service time did not solve the congregation's problems with religious education. As the church's Board of Education made plans for the fall of 1970, board members ran up against a significant failure in their efforts to secure teachers for Sunday school. Reasons for the failure were many, but they included the fact that a number of adults did not want to give up worship for a whole year in order to teach in a church school scheduled for the same time. The board even gave serious consideration for a while to abandoning Sunday school altogether.

But several board members took that major leap of faith which sees opportunity in the midst of adversity. If there was not enough interest or personnel to carry on the crafts class or the church school of the past, then why not try something new? Several persons did extensive study and research into new Christian education ventures in various other churches and denominations. Others borrowed from their knowledge of new developments in the world of secular education.

What emerged was the Experimental Church School, a program of essentially interest-oriented progressive education. Children from grades one to six were offered a choice from among a series of "short courses," each of which might last for as little as a month at a time. Courses were built around the interests of children and the interests of persons willing to teach—and many more adults were prepared to commit a month of their time to church school than to sign up from September to June.

A letter from the Board of Education to the congregation in the early fall of 1970 expressed the mood of the experimental program in the following appeal for teachers:

> You may feel that your interest does not tie in with Christian education or that you are not a teacher—but stamp collecting has been used to stir interest in second-graders as to our missions in other countries of our world—commemorative stamps have led to studies of great people and events with religious meaning—archaeology has interested students in the study of Palestine and the Dead Sea Scrolls.

Classes in this program were designed to bring together children of similar interests even if these children were in different grades in public school. Teachers were encouraged to involve the children actively in the process of learning rather than to give a lecture presentation to a young audience which was expected to sit quietly and listen. The child's self-expression was an important goal; it was hoped that self-expression might release the child's related ability to express and to share his or her faith with others.

Year-long denominational curricula were moved to the back library shelf to be used primarily as occasional resource or reference material. Other denominational literature geared toward shorter time periods, however, became more directly useful for monthly planning and weekly teaching. Several persons with particular talent created their own courses. And to give some larger vision and order to the diverse interests of a varied congregation, the Board of Education developed overall common themes to unify the course offerings in its experimental program.

There is much to affirm in the experimental church school, a program created largely through lay initiative and dedication. Behind the particular details were a welcome faith commitment, a spirit of adventure and risk, a desire to make the church a better place in which children may live and grow. The church had no thought at this time of the later developments which tried to integrate worship, education, and celebration. But much of the raw material for that three-part program, particularly for the education and the celebration periods, came out of the research and experience of the experimental church school.

A Separate Church and Church School

The most serious problem with the 1970 interest-oriented church school was not so much a difficulty within that program itself as it was a problem in the way the program related to the total life of South Church. Something new and exciting was happening inside the church school, but that school was isolated from and unrelated to the rest of the church. Church and church school were separate, and this separation made it difficult for the one to understand and accept something new in the other.

The existence of church and church school as parallel and unrelated institutions is far from a problem in South Church alone. Robert Lynn and Elliott Wright have written that

> Scores upon scores of Sunday schools in urban and rural areas function, as they always have, in relative separation from the rest of the church. "Sunday school is Sunday school" and "church is church" and in western Nebraska and on Tennessee's Cumberland Plateau one can skip the latter but not the former if social respectability is to be maintained. Given the tensions which have existed between Sunday school and congregation, superintendent and pastor, it is somewhat amazing that the educational program has survived at all.[1]

The institutional separation may take various forms. One common pattern is the assumption that worship is for adults and Christian education is for children. The child may grow up with little sense of belonging to the adult world of church; on graduation from the Sunday school, he or she may simply drop out of participation in the life of the parish. Adults, on the other hand, may feel little sense of involvement in the Christian education program, and a church has difficulty developing a strong interest in adult education.

For South Church in the fall of 1970, the separation of church and church school served to magnify the tensions in the total life of the parish. People could draw from a large pool of congregational turmoil—controversial social action, a change in the hour of worship, a decreased church school attendance. And now there was an experimental church school of progressive education. A tense parish found itself looking at an experimental program from the outside. Many had considerable difficulty trying to understand what was going on, let alone trying to incorporate that innovation into the ongoing life of the parish.

The adults who were not teaching that fall were involved in worship while the experimental program was taking place. The only contact that many had with the program was what they could hear—and on occasion they heard quite a bit. Children who are actively engaged in the learning process make noise. And an old church building is not as soundproof as it might be.

Add to the noise disturbance the initial impression of some parents that the experimental church school had abandoned "Bible-centered Christian education," and you have the formula for serious tensions within the congregation. Looking back, one can see that the attempt of the experimental program to build on the interests of children and teachers meant that many courses did not *sound like* the kind of classes people might expect in a Sunday school. On occasion the school may well have overreacted against traditional Christian education (as board members understood it); some courses may well have tried so hard to relate to children's interests that they never were able to find clear and significant ways to relate these interests to religious concerns. On many more occasions, church school teachers were able to make important tie-ins between children's interests and religious faith; but an upset church did not always hear, or listen for, these successes.

Adults who were not involved in the experimental program of Christian education began to talk about that program as something "they" were doing. Those who were excited by the innovation started to speak of congregational opposition in terms of "them," too. We were polarized and stalemated.

Out of that time of trial, however, a few came to realize that the valuable insights and experience of the experimental program could live over the long run only if the church could find a way to integrate the essence of that program into the totality of its life. Polarization within the church stood as an obstacle to any lasting growth in educational programs and to any deepening of the life and faith of the community of people who comprised South Church.

Take any imaginative and dedicated group of people who are caught up in a period of turmoil and introduce a new program into one isolated segment of that group, and you are likely to run into trouble. The natural focus of attention for criticism and defense in such a situation is usually the new program. But the deeper solution to people's problems is hardly to be found in rejecting that program or those who dislike it. Somehow the total group of people needs to find a way to overcome the barriers that isolate one segment of that group from another.

Out of stress, then, came a growing recognition within South Church that we could no longer afford the luxury of separation between church and church school. Few, if any, had a desire to go back to the days of crafts class—even if it had been possible to recover the customs and the mood of parish life in the early 1960s. People wanted to move forward, not backward. But before we look at the direction the congregation actually took, we need to touch on the worship background of South Church, as well as its Christian education program.

Two Kinds of Worship

A brainstorming group on the goals and beliefs of South Church at the end of the 1960s had tried to encourage "new as well as continuing traditional forms of worship." This group had suggested ways to "enliven our services and bring about greater participation of all members, young and old." Hopefully, they stated, the church could incorporate "the content and form of social action into the areas of worship and education." The goals and beliefs report even made the intriguing suggestion that the Board of Deacons "explore the possibility of celebrating Communion in the midst of the coffee hour which has become a happy extension of our Sunday worship, as well as in the regular service of worship."

Behind the formation of the brainstorming group one can see two groups of people in the congregation, attracted to two different kinds of corporate worship. One group liked the regular pattern of South Church worship, a pattern similar to most Protestant services today: scripture and sermon, choral music and hymns, prayer and an offering. A second group looked for a warm, open, spontaneous sharing between persons as an essential part of the worship experience.

The first group had a strong feeling of uneasiness about experimentation in worship. For them, contemporary services often lacked spiritual depth and balance. Such services tended to transform a worshiping congregation into a gathering of spectators for a performance put on by someone else. Conventional Protestant worship was meaningful for them as it was; why change it?

The second group welcomed all the change they could get in worship, feeling that a conventional service was often dull, lifeless, and irrelevant. Formal rituals seemed meaningless or repressive to them. How can you worship when you are sitting passively in one of a number of pews set up in rows so that all you can see is the back of people's heads in front of you? Couldn't we gather in a way that allowed us to see each other face to face during the service? And, if we felt moved to do so, why couldn't we clap our hands or tap our feet as a part of the worship of Almighty God?

South Church tried to meet the wishes of this latter group by turning over the regular morning service on occasion to specially planned contemporary services. The deacons also tried to develop a separate weekly contemporary worship experience at a time other than eleven o'clock. An early morning family service in the chapel was tried for a time. Usually, however, efforts at developing a second weekly service geared toward spontaneous sharing suffered from relatively small attendance and from periodically dwindling enthusiasm.

The debate between two groups in South Church over the nature of worship is hardly limited to that one congregation. Over and over, people in a variety of churches and denominations have struggled over two opposing concepts of what worship is. One point of view uses terms such as *formal* and *traditional;* the other uses words like *informal* and *spontaneous*. And it is difficult to please both groups of people in the same service.

Worship too, then, was an area of some tension in South Church. Some people recognized that we were dealing with two different kinds of corporate religious experience—what we would later describe as "worship" and "celebration." The question, however, was whether we would have to make a choice between these two, or whether we might find a way to make room for both in our regular Sunday morning church life.

1971—An Open-Ended Evaluation

In January of 1971, two months after arriving in Middletown, I made the proposal at a congregational meeting that we spend the coming year in a church-wide reevaluation. If there were signs of tension and turmoil within the parish, it was important to find the source of that turmoil. We needed to know where we were as a church and how we had gotten to that point; then, perhaps, we might be able to see clearly our direction for the future. The congregational meeting approved the proposal and established three lay committees to evaluate program, finances, and organizational structure.

The evaluation year was a significant leap of faith. Whatever the tensions and the strains within the church, people were able to agree on a process designed to lay those tensions out in the open, no holds barred. No one, myself included, had any idea at the beginning of the year of a three-part Sunday morning program of worship, education, and celebration. But we took the risk together of trusting that the Spirit would guide us from where we were to where we needed, and where we were able, to go in the years ahead.

A number of important reforms were implemented during 1971. After drafts and revisions and revisions of revisions, the congregation adopted a new constitution and bylaws by unanimous vote in December. The new structure gave added responsibility to the congregation as a whole to participate in the important decisions of the church. Lines of responsibility between boards and committees and staff members were clarified to reduce unnecessary ambiguity and conflict. We decided to balance a concern for the safety of principal and the rate of return in our invested funds with a concern for the social impact and the church involvement possible in the projects in which our money was to be invested.

The program evaluation committee groped its way toward an overview of the life of the parish. Committee members studied the experimental church school and its progressive, interest-oriented religious education. The committee also met with the Board of Deacons to evaluate the worship life of the church and to see how this area could be deepened for the whole membership of the parish.

I believe that South Church would not have been able to develop a wholistic program of worship, education, and celebration without something like that year-long, across-the-board evaluative process. By the fall of 1971 the strains and polarization within the church were healing, and the congregation as a whole was able to think about new forms of parish life. At least at the level of dreams for the future, we were moving beyond the image of a divided congregation and a compartmentalized program to the vision of an integrated church family able to welcome rich diversity and creativity within it.

A New Sunday Morning Program

In November of 1971, the Board of Deacons wrote a letter to the Board of Education asking for a joint meeting of the two boards along with the program evaluation committee to discuss the possibility of rescheduling the Sunday morning pattern of simultaneous church and church school. Deacons expressed the hope that we might find a new program which would allow the entire church, young and old, to be able to participate in a vital experience of both worship and education.

The three groups met on December 2. Some suggested the long-time South Church pattern of church school first and worship second, giving us the opportunity to "tie the loose ends of the morning together" in a closing worship period. Another group felt that worship should come at the beginning of the morning when people were least tired; the service would then serve as a common starting point for young and old.

One woman (who in 1973 came to serve as part-time Christian education coordinator for South Church) brought in a proposal for a two-hour program in three parts: a period of worship at the beginning, followed by a period of Christian education, followed by a closing worship time. This proposal touched off the major discussion of the evening.

Some of those present felt that putting education "in the middle of" worship would destroy the meaning of a service. But as we played with the idea of a three-part Sunday morning program, we started to see that it was not necessary to think about "destroying the integrity of worship" as though we were "cutting worship in half." It was possible, instead, to think about a three-part Sunday morning program which placed

Christian education in between two different kinds of worship experience, each with its own separate integrity. The idea of one service in three acts was born.

Slowly, the three-part service idea captured the imaginations of the persons at that important meeting. If scripture and sermon were placed in the opening worship, the congregation could respond to the intellectual challenge of these elements when people were least tired. And if there were a closing worship experience of some kind, it would be possible then to draw the church back together before people separated for the coming week. Rather than choose between starting with worship and ending with worship, why not do both? There would still be an opportunity in between the two worship periods for a program of Christian education for all ages.

The December 2 meeting reached the consensus that the idea of a two-hour service in three acts was worth further exploration. Yet the large group at that session was unable to refine the proposal, to fill in the details, to provide an underlying rationale which could give final shape to a workable program. The meeting adjourned with a sense of some progress and of considerable unfinished business.

A Theology or Rationale for the New Program

During the next few days, I worked out a further proposal that we build a two-hour, three-part service on the model of a service of Holy Communion (the Eucharist, the Lord's Supper, the Mass). Down through the ages of the Christian church, Holy Communion has traditionally been composed of two parts: a service of the Word, and a service of the Sacrament. It would be both possible and relatively easy to make the opening act of the Sunday morning program a service of the Word. The closing act could be a kind of expanded service of the Sacrament, in which we celebrated the presence of Christ not only in the bread and the wine, but in the whole of life. With a period of Christian education for all ages in between these two experiences of worship, we would have a three-act service of worship, education, and celebration.

"The Word" in a theology of worship usually refers specifically to scripture and sermon. The first act, as a service of the Word, would develop a complete worship experience around scripture and sermon by adding such elements as prayer, music, an offering. Such a service is essentially what most people probably think of as conventional Protestant worship.

The second act in the two-hour program would be the education period. At the conclusion of act one, there would be a brief intermission to give people of all ages time to go to classes of their choice. These classes would have their own beginning and ending, their own integrity, just as the service of the Word would have its own completeness. Teachers could follow a denominational curriculum or develop their own courses, as they and the Board of Education felt possible and appropriate. But the education period would also serve a new function in helping to digest the content of the opening worship act and in helping to prepare people for the closing celebration time.

The final act of the three-part service, the celebration period, would build on the theological foundations of the service of the Sacrament. We could, however, celebrate the broken body of Christ, not only in the broken bread of the Eucharist, but also in the pain and suffering of a broken world. The congregation could celebrate the new life Christ gives, not only in the shared cup of wine or grape juice as the new covenant in his blood; the new life of Christ could be celebrated in such varied events today as healing, forgiveness, peace, baptism, justice, hope.

Celebration would be a time in which we could look at significant areas of our life and attempt together to lift up the faith meaning they may convey. Common objects seen through the eyes of faith could become symbols through which Christ can enter our lives. Significant events in the life of the church or the world could be seen as parables of faith which help people understand the Kingdom of God. Our relationships could be affirmed as windows through which we see God's love.

This climactic period of the Sunday morning program must have an element of spontaneity and informality if the church is to be truly open to the consecrating presence of the Holy Spirit. The celebration period as described above could fulfill the needs and hopes of persons who are looking for warm, personal, sharing worship. It would not be easy, and it would probably take abundant patience to allow people the time and the freedom to learn how to celebrate. But this final act could find its own integrity as a complete experience and yet help to bring the whole three-part service to a close as the climax of the morning.

The entire two-hour service could be diagramed in the form of a spiral. The congregation begins with an experience of worship and moves out through a time of religious education. As people come back to a concluding worship period, to celebration, they discover that they have moved to a new level. Celebration is simply worship at another level than the conventional opening service. The church is involved in three separate acts, but as its members progress through these acts they pass from one level of involvement to another.

Each act, then, would have its own beginning and ending, its own sense of value and integrity in and of itself. A person could come to any one act alone and hope to get something out of that act. But the whole three-part service would be greater than the sum of its parts. Each act would also take on new meaning in relation to the larger Sunday morning program.

What I was looking for in the above rationale for a three-part service was a way of integrating separate components in a church's life without destroying the essence of each of those components. The purpose was not to merge or blend worship and education and celebration into a single composite experience. The goal was integration, not amalgamation.

Practical Refinements

Some of the South Church debates in the days which followed focused on the theology or rationale of the new Sunday morning program. The program evaluation committee in particular wrestled in this area. There were other proposals, other ways of thinking through a three-part service. But the substance of the above theology gradually gained enough support to enable us to proceed along its general lines. What remained to be done was the attempt to work out enough practical details within the overall theology for us to implement a workable program.

The opening worship act emerged relatively unchanged from the pattern of worship that the church was familiar with from its past history. The service was shortened to about forty-five minutes in order to allow enough time for the other two acts. The decision to provide basic continuity in the formal worship pattern of South Church has helped immeasurably in the long-term goal of winning the congregation's acceptance and approval for the whole three-part service. Most people have been willing to allow for something new on Sunday morning as long as they can also find the kinds of experience they found valuable in the past.

The new program required a shortening in the time available for Christian education. Despite the fact that education was scheduled for 10:50 and celebration for 11:40, the inevitable stragglers meant that some classes had less productive classroom time than they might have wished. Some still find this reduction in time for religious education to be the most serious drawback of the three-part service. On the other hand, if the two-hour program cut back the amount of time available for the education of children, it opened up the opportunity for substantial adult education; instead of leaving adults in church while children went to church school, the new program provided classes for all ages once the opening service was over.

Celebration was set for about twenty minutes on the average. That period of time has proved to be long enough to allow significant events to happen as the congregation gathers to celebrate week in and week out. Yet twenty minutes is also short enough for people not to be overly upset if little or nothing of significance happens on a particular Sunday and things fall flat on their face. On special Sundays the congregation has been quite willing to postpone Sunday dinner a little while to allow for a longer celebration.

The overall time limit of two hours reflects several practical concerns. The church wanted to keep the total time short enough to let the majority of people in the congregation feel willing and able to make a commitment to attend the three acts; our experience since the program was implemented has been that about two-thirds of those who come at ten o'clock stay all the way through. Families with small children felt that two hours was the maximum time they could expect their children to last for a Sunday morning church program. Yet two hours seemed long enough to develop three complete acts. There was even the hope that each act would stop when interest and excitement were highest, thus building people's interest for the overall experience.

Significantly, one of the comments heard most often from South Church members as we moved from a one-hour program of simultaneous church and church school to a two-hour program of worship, education, and celebration was the plea "We don't have enough time." If that is the kind of criticism a church gets, it must be doing something right.

One major variation in schedule should be mentioned here. The two-hour program at South Church has not replaced the particular service of Holy Communion. On the first Sunday of each month, the church celebrates the Lord's Supper. There are no education classes that Sunday, which gives the Christian education program a monthly break in between courses. Following the service of Communion (a service of Word and Sacrament), the congregation moves to the social room for an informal coffee hour which completes the morning.

Gradually, as the congregation moved into January of 1972, the practical details were settled. Some of the arguments had humorous overtones. One person felt that there were strong theological reasons for placing the morning offering in the third act of the three-part service, the celebration period. He may well have been right. But others protested that there would be more people present during the opening worship period than in celebration, and that we would get more money in the plates if the offering were left in the first act. The practical reasons won out, and the theology had to be adjusted accordingly.

A Beginning

In February of 1972, three years after changing the Sunday morning service time from eleven to ten o'clock, the South Congregational Church began its new two-hour program of worship, education, and celebration. We had worked out enough theory and practice for the parish to be ready to implement its ideas and to learn from experience.

Following an initial trial period, the congregation conducted a thorough and extensive review of the three-act service on May 8 of that year. By that time we had uncovered a few minor problems which needed adjustment. We also listened to a variety of criticisms, some that the new program was too liberal and others that it was too conservative. After hearing all the comments, however, people realized that many of the criticisms simply cancelled each other out, in effect.

At the end of that May 8 review session, each board or committee which was present and involved in the implementation of the three-act service voted separately to continue that service as our regular Sunday morning program for the indefinite future. All recognized tremendous room for growth ahead. But the congregation made the basic decision to do its growing within an integrated program of worship, education, and celebration. That decision has shaped the church's life ever since.

Ultimately, offering a variety of three different kinds of experience within a single Sunday morning program is an effort to celebrate diversity. And yet the attempt to integrate these experiences in one program is an attempt to reconcile the diverse people who participate in that program. One service in three acts, then, is a direct programmatic reflection of the existence of one church in three parts.

A Christmas Pageant

It has always been easiest to describe the three-part service by means of illustrations. A few months after the Vietnam Sunday described at the beginning of this chapter, South Church decided to put on a Christmas pageant—the dramatic presentation of the biblical story of Jesus' birth as we find it in Luke and Matthew. But the pageant was shaped in unique ways by the church's two-hour program.

The sermon on the first Sunday of December, 1972, was centered on Jesus' statement "Truly, I say to you, unless you turn and become like children, you will never enter the kingdom of heaven" (Matthew 18:3). After an introduction on that passage, the minister asked the congregation how many were familiar with Christmas pageants—with Mary and Joseph and the baby Jesus, with shepherds and wise men and angels, with the crowded inn and the stable and manger behind it. Almost everybody raised his or her hand in the affirmative.

The minister went on to propose in that sermon that we act out a Christmas pageant in South Church during a celebration period later that month. Two suggestions, however, would distinguish that pageant from the kind of performance that most churches expect during the Christmas season.

First was the suggestion that everybody, young and old, participate in the celebration pageant. The familiar pattern is a performance of the Christmas story put on by the children for the adults. But South Church had been trying to involve the whole church family in worship and education and celebration. Why not invite that whole family, all ages, to participate in the pageant?

Jesus' words in that morning's scripture lesson reminded us that becoming like children helped us to be able to enter the kingdom of heaven. Part of what he may have been referring to is the ability of children to play a story, to enter into a tale and play different roles or characters, letting these characters come alive in them in fresh and spontaneous ways. If all of us were free to become like children in our participation in a dramatic reenactment of the familiar Christmas story, we might come to understand more fully in our own experience what Jesus meant.

The second suggestion was that we put on a Christmas pageant without rehearsal. The point of celebration is not for one group to put on a performance for others to watch, but for all of us to participate in the experience of celebrating for the sake of living into it. There was, therefore, no final performance for which we would have to rehearse; or, to put it another way, the celebration pageant could be described as the dress rehearsal, the one and only rehearsal we would have, with no final performance to follow.

The congregation would need some structure for a pageant. The familiarity of the biblical story itself would provide the basic structure. Beyond that, a celebration narrator would be appointed in advance whose task would be to tell the Christmas story during the pageant and to help organize people's creativity on the spot.

There would also be a sign-up sheet on the bulletin board with room for individuals or groups to sign up for whatever parts they wished to play in the drama. As long as all the important parts were covered and there was no unnecessary duplication of roles, the church would be able to reenact the biblical story of Jesus' birth as we went along. Within the familiar narrative, we could find ample room for spontaneity and imagination as the congregation lived into the characters and let the story come alive in us.

Christian education courses that Advent had been arranged around what were called "family project groups." There were eight different groups, each composed of sixteen or so persons of varying ages. A sample group might have two young couples with their children, an older couple whose children had left home, a widow, a bachelor, a woman who came alone because her husband was not interested in church. Each group was a kind of extended family, providing a supportive atmosphere during the holiday season to everyone who wanted to participate—an important experience in particular for those who had no family of their own.

The project groups picked up on the idea of the Christmas pageant. One group signed up immediately to be the angels and prepared to sing a series of carols up in the sanctuary balcony—the "highest heaven" of the biblical story. A second group spent its time making simple gifts, such as a bird feeder. These gifts were given to the wise men to bring forward as the "gold" or "frankincense" or "myrrh" for the baby Jesus; after the pageant, the bird feeder was given to an elderly woman living next door to the church as a herald of spring.

One class worked out a special script for the end of the pageant, involving interviews with various witnesses to the birth asking these persons what that birth meant to them. A fourth group scouted up costumes for the major characters in the drama, looking through attics of the church building and the homes of various church members; with needle and thread and glue, these costumes were made ready.

Not every group focused all its time or energy on the celebration pageant. Some sang Christmas carols during an education period at the state mental hospital nearby. Others studied the meaning of the Christmas passages in Luke and Matthew, with an opportunity for children to draw pictures of various portions of the story. Even for groups which branched out from an exclusive focus on the pageant, however, the fact of that coming celebration experience provided a climate of high expectancy in the whole parish.

Individual persons prepared for the pageant, too. A seven-year-old boy signed up to be Joseph and spent time at home cutting down and whittling a staff to use as he walked down the aisle with Mary looking for lodging. One young couple in the church decided to have their baby girl baptized on the Sunday of the pageant; the baptism took place during the opening worship, but the baby was consecrated later that morning in a special way by becoming the baby Jesus in the celebration drama. The minister chose to be a sheep, claiming that the job of shepherd in a congregation needed to be passed around on occasion.

The Christmas pageant was celebrated on the third Sunday of Advent. It was an amazing experience. There were moments of real beauty, such as the music sung by the angels in the balcony. Three teen-agers showed ingenuity by hiding behind a pew and shining their flashlights on the sanctuary ceiling to represent the star the wise men followed to Bethlehem. The climactic moment for many was the feeling of deep worship as the narrator looked at the baby Jesus and said with both spontaneity and sincerity, "Isn't Jesus beautiful!"

The atmosphere in that celebration also reflected moods that some people found unfamiliar in a worship experience. Most people heartily enjoyed themselves; it is an important commentary on that celebration to see the number of smiles on people's faces in the pictures that were taken that Sunday. The pageant touched on melodrama as Herod came strutting up the aisle and the congregation responded with a spontaneous hissing. And children were free to ask questions about what was happening as the story progressed; the congregation incorporated the questions and the answers into the developing drama instead of telling children to wait quietly until everything was all over before they could talk.

Questions for the Future

The vast majority of the church came away from that pageant with warm feelings and good memories. A few, however, did not. One of the significant factors in the total experience of that celebration drama was what happened afterward. The majority tried to listen to those who had difficulty with the pageant and, without giving up their own good memories, came to recognize that there was something important in the questions a few were asking.

There had been an explicit attempt to make a distinction between having fun in the biblical story, which we welcomed, and making fun of the story, which the congregation obviously wanted to avoid. Given inevitable human limitations and the necessary risks in an unrehearsed celebration, most people thought that we were amazingly successful in following through on that distinction. A handful, however, felt that we were not always as reverent as a church should be. Did the pageant show the kind of respect to stories from the Holy Bible which these stories demand?

The more people lived with the experience of the Christmas pageant, the more we realized the importance of working out a deeper understanding of reverence. What are appropriate and respectful ways to live into biblical stories? It may be acceptable to most people to have fun in portions of the story of Jesus' birth. But what do we do with some of the other stories in the biblical record?

How, for example, would a congregation deal in a celebration period with the biblical story of the slaughter of the innocents in Matthew 2:16-18? This story is also a part of the background in Jesus' birth and it sets that birth in the middle of the tragedy of human existence. What are reverent ways to let the stories of Lent and Easter come alive in a celebration experience? How does a congregation celebrate suffering and death—or is that goal possible or even desirable?

The ongoing celebration life of South Church has grown to include more and more biblical material. With that growth the church has moved beyond the Christmas pageant of 1972. It was important to experience together the fun in that particular drama, but we have come to realize the need for celebration periods to touch deeper levels in our human history as well.

Yet the Christmas pageant was a breakthrough in the three-part Sunday morning program. During that pageant many people began to feel the possibilities in a celebration period in a way they had not before. The congregation also sensed the possibilities in integrating the three different acts of the Sunday service. As the Christmas pageant entered the storehouse of the church's accumulated experience, the congregation had the distinct sense that something memorable had happened and that the course we had chosen was good.

A history, a vision, the structure of one service in three acts, a few moving experiences—these are important. But if the vision is to be shared in a way that may allow others to enter into it in their own ways with their own helpful variations on a theme, we need to look in greater depth at each of the three parts of that Sunday morning program and at the purpose and implications of the total experience.

2
Worship

Some nineteen hundred years ago in the city of Corinth, in what is now Greece, a newly formed church congregation ran into problems in its worship. One person seemed to feel that God had given him the particular gift of wisdom or knowledge; he was sure as a result that the most important thing in worship was that it convey wisdom and knowledge to the congregation. Another apparently possessed the more exotic gift of speaking in tongues or prophesying; she was convinced accordingly that her gift was much more dramatic evidence of the presence of God than mere mundane wisdom.

The average worshiper in that parish may well have found himself or herself caught in a tug-of-war between two concepts of worship. When St. Paul, the founder of the congregation, was able to write a pastoral letter to the church, he included the words "For, in the first place, when you assemble as a church, I hear that there are divisions among you" (1 Corinthians 11:18).

Paul was clear in affirming the variety of gifts in that Corinthian congregation. The diversity of the membership may have threatened the overall unity of the congregation, but he had no interest in trying to press people into a uniform mold as a means of preserving a superficial harmony. His letters urge that the church allow for the expression of a variety of gifts. Each of the gifts, however, is rooted in the one Spirit of Christ Jesus. Every church member is a part of the one body of Christ. The unity of Christ allows room for diversity within it.

In the fourteenth chapter of 1 Corinthians, Paul deals more specifically with the problems of worship in a diverse congregation. His thought suggests that there are two basic elements in worship: *order* and *spirit*. Both must be present in any vital worship, though they exist in continual tension with each other.

On the one hand, Paul explicitly encourages such esoteric gifts of the Spirit as prophecy and speaking in tongues; he wishes to keep worship open to the power of the spontaneous life of the Spirit. On the other hand, Paul recognizes that people can be carried away into divisive and unhealthy excesses when they open themselves in an undisciplined, unknowing way to that life of the Spirit. There must always be a rational element of order in worship to balance the element of spirit. A recognized order can shape diverse spiritual gifts so that they serve to strengthen the overall life and unity of the church.

In what may be the earliest written record we have of the kind of order of worship used in the early Christian church, Paul writes: "What then, brethren? When you come together, each one has a hymn, a lesson, a revelation, a tongue, or an interpretation. Let all things be done for edification. . . . So, my brethren, earnestly desire to prophesy, and do not forbid speaking in tongues; but all things should be done decently and in order" (1 Corinthians 14:26, 39-40).

Spirit, then, is related to the vitality of worship, yet too much raw spirit can lead to chaos or unwanted excesses. Some order is necessary to channel that spirit in beneficial ways. Yet too much order can be a problem, too, in that such order can stifle living spirit and lead to rigid, cold, and unfeeling worship.

Worship is like fire. Fire can warm us. It can cook our food. Yet too much fire can burn buildings and destroy people. Fire needs to be channeled in a fireplace or a stove or a furnace for it to be beneficial. A fire can go out, however, if it is stifled in an enclosed area without air and without room to burn freely. Worship, as fire, needs to be channeled but not stifled if it is to meet our hopes and needs.

Historical Worship Patterns

The Christian church has developed a variety of worship patterns down through its history. Looking at that variety one sees that it is probably impossible to create a pattern which is either pure order or pure spirit. It is more useful to picture a spectrum of worship patterns running from order at one end to spirit at the other. Each has its own particular tension between order and spirit, though some patterns emphasize order over spirit and others do the reverse.

Evelyn Underhill in her classic book *Worship* sheds helpful light on the nature and varieties of worship in the wider church. The book opens with a basic definition: "Worship, in all its grades and kinds, is the response of the creature to the Eternal. . . . For worship is an acknowledgment of Transcendence; that is to say, of a Reality independent of the worshipper, which is always more or less deeply coloured by mystery, and which is there first."[1]

One of the ways by which humankind expresses its need for order in worship is in the development of rituals: "powerful instruments, whereby the worshipping temper is taught, stimulated, and maintained. . . . So, too, the ritual chant, with its accompaniment of ceremonial movement and manual acts, is found to exert a stabilizing influence at every level of his religious life." But too much concern for order, at the expense of spirit, can lead to the danger of ritualism, that stifling state where we "assume that the precise way in which things are done is of supreme importance, and that the traditional formula has an inherent authority extending to its smallest details, from which it is blasphemy to depart."[2]

Free church worship, on the other hand, generally places an emphasis on spirit, "leaving room for the expression of that prophetic, ethical, spontaneous element in the primitive Christian response to God, which every reform and revival seeks to restore." Such a pattern of worship is "suspicious of set forms, and demands a spontaneous worship which shall be the devotional expression of a personal and subjective relation to God." Too much concern for spirit, however, at the expense of order, can lead to "the tendency to exaggeration and to lawless individualism which dogs all inspirational worship."[3]

History and our own experience are filled with examples of worship patterns at both ends of the spectrum. Patterns emphasizing order include high church worship and formal liturgies, well-rehearsed choirs that process and recess, litanies and printed responses. The life of the Spirit, however, receives more emphasis in low church worship and extemporaneous prayers, in hymn sings and testimonial services, in a revival or a Quaker meeting or a Pentecostal service.

Underhill's book is useful in its descriptions of the variety of worship experiences one can find within the church. Moreover, she expresses the important thesis that a mature worship life needs the richness both of patterns which emphasize order and of those which emphasize spirit.

> Habit and attention must therefore co-operate in the life of worship; and it is a function of cultus to maintain this vital partnership. Habit alone easily deteriorates into mechanical repetition, the besetting sin of the liturgical mind. Attention alone means, in the end, intolerable strain. Each partner has his weak point. Habit tends to routine and spiritual red-tape; the vice of the institutionalist. Attention is apt to care for nothing but the experience of the moment, and ignore the need of a stable practice, independent of personal fluctuations; the vice of the individualist. Habit is a ritualist. Attention is a pietist. But it is the beautiful combination of order and spontaneity, docility and freedom, living humbly—and therefore fully and freely—within the agreed pattern of the cultus and not in defiance of it, which is the mark of a genuine spiritual maturity and indeed the fine flower of a worshipping life.[4]

If, however, there is value in providing space in one's worship life for both order and spirit, Underhill expresses the belief that it is particularly difficult to mix such widely different kinds of experience. Those who prefer formal, ordered worship have often seen themselves in conflict with those who prefer a freer pattern of worship—and vice versa. This conflict is rooted not so much in personal stubbornness (though that may be a factor on occasion) as in the wide divergence between the two experiences.

> There is here, of course, a marked difference of ideal between the conceptions of "free" and "ordered" worship: the extempore prayer meeting where all make their personal contribution, and there is unreserved expression of individual aspirations and needs, and the grave movement of the Divine Service, with its note of impersonal objectivity, the subordination of individual fervour to the total adoring act. . . . These completing opposites, both present in the primitive Church, are both needed if the full span and possibilities of Christian worship are to be realized; and it is one of the many tragedies of Church history that they have so often been regarded as hostile to one another. . . . Nevertheless it seems as though in practice the two types were better kept apart. Modern attempts to combine them in one service; e.g. by means of "biddings" in the Eucharist, or the addition of non-liturgic prayers in the daily office, make great demands on the liturgical tact of those who venture on these perilous experiments. The enrichment of Free Church services by carefully chosen liturgical forms is more easily managed; but here, too, the harmonizing of the different kinds of material is a matter needing considerable skill.[5]

This brief look at Evelyn Underhill's book on *worship* is valuable as background for the way in which the worship experience of one particular modern parish fits into the larger worship developments of the wider church. When people in the South Congregational Church of Middletown were looking for a worship period which emphasized order and a celebration period emphasizing spirit, we were joining in a much larger search of congregations and individuals down through the centuries.

The final decision in South Church to initiate a three-part program of worship and education and celebration is hardly grounds to claim that this congregation has arrived at "genuine spiritual maturity"—to use Underhill's words. We have taken only a couple of steps. We do believe, however, that our goal of allowing for both an ordered worship experience and a freer celebration within our weekly church life together sets us in the right direction.

Underhill's book is also important in reminding us of the sharp distinctions between different kinds of worship. A pattern at one end of the spectrum which emphasizes order over spirit can be radically different from a second pattern at the other end which emphasizes spirit over order. It may well be important to provide for both kinds of worship in our religious life, yet it can be exceedingly difficult to combine these two kinds in a genuine way in a single weekly church service. The three-part Sunday morning program with formal worship separated from informal celebration by Christian education classes may be one significant way to preserve the distinctiveness of two kinds of worship within an overall integrated program.

Modern Criticisms of Formal and Informal Worship

The categories of order and spirit developed above provide a framework within which to look at some modern criticisms of church worship. It is not hard today to find someone who is willing to criticize formal worship as dry, dull, lifeless, and irrelevant. Critics caricature such worship as a collection of hypocrites who come to a large and forbidding room to sit as passive spectators to a strange and ancient performance that they will forget about as soon as it is over.

Some of those who criticize have difficulty with the whole experience of the worship of God. Others have difficulty with the inevitable human limitations of the worshiping congregation or its leaders. But a considerable number of critics simply feel that there is too much order and too little spirit in the experience. This latter group is really asking for a different kind of experience, a more spirited worship, at the other end of the spectrum.

The problem comes from the unhappy fact that those who criticize formal worship may be far more aware of the defects in an ordered service than they are aware of the comparable defects in a service of spirit and informality. Spontaneous worship has its critics too, however.

There is no way of opening worship to spontaneity without accepting a certain amount of risk as to what happens as a result of that spontaneity. A freer service is much more open to extremes than one which is planned to follow a standard order week after week. Paul's words in 1 Corinthians remind us of the potential divisiveness in a spirit-filled service with no fundamental discipline and order to hold things together.

There may be value in opening the door to unplanned experiences, but there is no reason to expect that human beings will automatically respond to that open door by spontaneously sharing the full richness of biblical faith. Individuals and congregations inevitably find some portions of the gospel which speak to them and other portions which do not. Given the opportunity of open sharing, people share far more naturally out of those portions of faith which are meaningful to them than out of those which seem irrelevant. The content of a service which emphasizes spirit over order is often shaped, therefore, not so much by the full biblical story as by our own experience. And if limited human experience comes to exercise a veto over what happens in worship, we may well end up with an oversimplified view of the nature of faith.

Once again, the critics of spontaneous worship may be far more aware of the good points in ordered worship than they are aware of the bad. Critics of informal worship may look longingly at the balance, the perspective, the objectivity which are possible in an ordered service.

Formal worship provides the opportunity for intellectual depth in a sermon, whereas the tendency toward oversimplification in informal worship often makes such depth extremely difficult. With a regular weekly ordered service, a congregation can plan to cover the whole range of important doctrines of faith over the course of time. The device of a lectionary, for example, plans scripture readings over a year or more in such a way that the congregation is exposed to the full richness of biblical tradition. A doctrine which may seem to be irrelevant today may prove to be an important guide to a new experience which confronts us tomorrow.

Many congregations find themselves at a stand-off as they approach the question of how to find more meaning in their worship life. Some are satisfied with things as they are. Critics of formal worship often see the bad points in such worship and the good points in a more spontaneous experience; the critics of spontaneous services often see the reverse. The usual result is a stalemate and a decision by default to keep going the way the congregation always has.

If our brief look at St. Paul and at Evelyn Underhill was at all helpful, however, it may have suggested that the problems we are meeting in trying to make worship more meaningful are deep and long-standing. A congregation today which tries to make its worship more modern and relevant may be stymied in part by the basic difficulties churches have always had in trying to combine two radically different kinds of worship.

It may help for a while to take a formal service and fit in a guitar here and a contemporary reading there. But over the long run, these new elements may appear to be gimmicks which try to "jazz things up," rather than genuine attempts to deepen "the response of the creature to the Eternal" (to use Underhill's definition of worship). Some churches are beginning to discover that contemporary innovations in worship initiated a few years ago are already showing signs of wearing a bit thin.

Formal and Informal Worship: A Both-And

Behind the writing of this book is the belief that many problems in worship today cannot be solved as long as the church sees formal and spontaneous services to be an either-or. These two kinds of worship are complementary; they each gain when they become a both-and. Formal worship needs the presence of spontaneous services to provide life and vitality in the church's total worship. Spontaneous worship needs the presence of a formal service to give stability and balance.

Formal worship is like the rudder on a sailboat which helps to steer the craft and to keep it from being blown this way and that by changing gusts of wind. Informal worship is like the wind-filled sail which helps the boat to speed along the water. A sailboat needs both rudder and sail if it is to move in the direction we want it to go. Formal worship alone can be like a boat with a rudder and no sail: we are headed in the right direction, but we never move. Spontaneous worship alone can be like having a sail and no rudder: we are caught up in the excitement of skimming over the water, but because the boat is out of control it may easily tip over or run aground. A full worship life needs both the rudder of an ordered service and the sail of a spirited service.

Obviously, no pattern of worship is perfect. And changing one imperfect service to another may be of limited value. The attempt to integrate two kinds of services in the church's regular Sunday morning experience may enrich the total impact of worship, however. It takes time and patience for a congregation to learn to worship in two different ways. But the goal is worth the effort.

The Effect of Celebration on Worship

Before South Church adopted its three-part Sunday morning program, worship services were an uneasy compromise between the ordered and spontaneous. The three-act service allowed the congregation to separate out the two kinds of worship. The first act was free to be an experience of formal worship without attempting at the same time to meet the quite different needs of spontaneous worship. And informal, personal sharing was freed from having to fight for room inside the regular service when it found a home in celebration.

The three-act service, then, provides an interesting kind of innovation: the opening service is more formal, more standardized, more ordered than the regular service that many congregations have come to use. In the continuing effort to win and hold congregational acceptance of the new Sunday morning program, it has been of enormous value to be able to state that the new service stabilizes formal worship from week to week.

Stability is one of the goals that a congregation may legitimately expect from a pattern of worship emphasizing order over spirit. The church needs to keep from drifting around from fad to fad without any long-range sense of direction or motivation. Without a basic stability how can a congregation sustain difficult social action projects which require years of frustrating work? It was Jesus long ago who commended the wise man who built his house on the rock so that it would stand up against rain and wind and flood, against polarization and controversy and apathy.

When stability becomes the only goal of a congregation, however, parish life can easily degenerate into repressive rigidity, lifeless legalism. The regular presence of a celebration period at the end of the church's Sunday morning life together helps to sustain the continuing growth of the Spirit within the membership. Worship plus celebration equals stability plus growth.

A Youth Sunday

The complementary relationship between the first and third acts of the two-hour program is illustrated by the Youth Sunday service at South Church in May of 1973. Several high school students led the ten o'clock service within the standard order of worship which the congregation was used to following at that hour. The sermon was a series of five dramatic skits on different aspects of love in a variety of human situations. Each skit included a musical selection sung by one of the youth. Taken as a whole, the five skits gave a balanced picture of love in everyday life.

The young people also wanted to lead the celebration period

that morning. During act three they felt they could relax and be themselves in a way that was extremely difficult in act one. As the congregation regathered for the celebration time, the youth asked us to consecrate their sermon of the morning by learning one of the musical pieces from one of the five skits. People sat informally on the chancel steps, in the front pews, or even on the floor. Two young persons provided guitar accompaniment, and everyone joined in—with clapping of hands and tapping of feet and whatever other motions people felt moved to add.

Worship and celebration reinforced each other that particular day. Each had an importance in and of itself. But both experiences together provided a depth to the total Sunday morning service which would have been impossible had we been required to choose between formal and informal worship.

The youth had something that morning that they wanted to say to the congregation. Many of them felt that the formality of ordered worship was difficult and awkward. But the youth group as a whole decided to go along with that formality anyway. The group recognized that many adults in the church placed considerable importance on formal worship. If young people wanted adults to listen to them, the youth felt a responsibility to listen to what the adults wanted, too. Maybe older people could hear what youth had to say better if those youth could say it in a medium and a context which was familiar to the whole congregation and accepted by everyone.

By the time the church came to celebration, however, it became obvious that many of the young people really had their hearts in the kind of open, spontaneous experience which is possible in that third act. Without anyone saying it in so many words, the church seemed to feel that an implicit bargain of sorts had been struck between the youth and the adults: the youth were willing to participate in the formal worship which many adults found comfortable and familiar, and now the youth wanted and expected those adults to participate in the informal celebration which many youth found comfortable and familiar. There is some inaccurate stereotyping here; not every adult is comfortable with formality or every youth with informality. But the "implicit bargain" which many persons felt that morning gave added meaning to the total two-hour service.

The significant part of celebration that Sunday was that many older persons who were not comfortable with the informality of the occasion were able, nonetheless, to enter into the spirit of that act. No one had been asked to give up formal worship in order to share in this second experience. There were no angry "hidden agendas" floating around with one group trying to prove that informal worship was really better and another group trying to prove the opposite. The church as a whole had made the institutional decision to affirm two different kinds of worship experience as valid and legitimate when we adopted the three-part Sunday morning program.

In addition, much of the content of celebration seemed highly appropriate when it was done during that third act, though it would have been highly inappropriate during a formal service. The mode of congregational involvement in ordered worship is related to a sense of peace and quiet within which persons may touch the deepest levels of being, and experience the presence of God at those levels. Clapping hands and tapping feet may make it quite difficult for a person to "center down"—to use the Quaker expression for worship.

On the other hand, if it is appropriate for the congregation to seek a mood of quiet listening and deep meditation during act one, such a mood is quite out of place in celebration. The youth wanted the whole congregation to join in with them, to share in the experience that they had presented during the sermon. Quiet listening during celebration would have been interpreted as an unfriendly and an "uptight" rejection of the youth by the rest of the church.

Again, had we spent the entire sermon time in the opening service on one musical piece, many would have come away from the experience with the feeling that the sermon lacked intellectual depth and balance. There are so many different dimensions to the human experience of love that a single musical selection almost necessarily leaves us with a distorted picture of that experience. The sermon that morning, however, had actually included five selections on love; it was able to give an overall picture with some balance.

What the sermon did not provide was the fullest opportunity for the congregation to enter into the experience of worship. Listening to a well-developed presentation is important, but listening is not enough. There are other levels of involvement beyond listening which make it possible for the content of the sermon to come alive with far more power than through listening alone. When we move to these other levels of experience, people are not as concerned about balance as about opening the possibility of personal participation in at least a small part of what is happening.

The goal of that celebration, then, was not to present a repetition of the morning sermon. The youth were trying instead to involve the congregation in sharing a small part of the sermon experience so that each of us could more fully feel the spirit of love moving in her or him. In the course of two hours, the congregation was able to listen to a balanced presentation on love and to learn how to participate in a part of the experience of expressing that love.

The Youth Sunday illustration shows that formal worship has no need to become locked into such a rigid order that there is no room for spirit. A sermon with guitars and music and drama can be quite spirited; it is different from the usual spoken message from the pulpit. That sermon did fit into formal worship, however, because it was a genuine attempt to interpret scripture within a particular, accepted order of service.

By the same token, celebration cannot be pure spirit and no order. The youth wanted to teach the congregation the words and the tune of one song. In order to accomplish that task, they needed enough order in act three to be able to gather people together and get them to be relatively quiet for a period of time.

The advantage of having education classes in between act one and act three is in part that it allows both worship and celebration to develop their own distinctive style and integrity. When formal and informal worship are mixed together, one can easily end up with a "hodge-podge" experience of little depth, a "lowest common denominator" service which tries to please everybody but which actually compromises the deepest possibilities in the human experience of God's presence. Yet the separate acts of worship and celebration can still complement and reinforce each other. The total Sunday morning program has both unity and diversity.

Traditional Worship in Act One

When a congregation gathers for worship today, it is meeting within a given tradition which helps to define and shape who it is and how it acts. Fundamentally, every Christian parish gathers within the tradition of the whole church from biblical times down through the present. Each community of faith also comes together amid the particular traditions of branches of that church, reflecting the different worship patterns which various denominations and congregations have developed out of our common heritage.

Act one of the three-part service attempts to root the worship life of this Middletown congregation in the larger tradition of the church as well as in the traditions of the United Church of Christ and of this parish. A worshiping congregation meditates on deep issues, such as the meaning of life and death, or the nature of forgiveness and reconciliation; but the meditation takes place in the context of a rich history out of which people seek to define a sense of meaning. Christian worship does not occur in a vacuum or out of the blue. Our history and tradition as a part of the people of God are an important element in who we are when we gather to praise the Lord.

Formal worship tries to ground our life in a valuable tradition. But worship should not be imprisoned by tradition. Congregations are in trouble if we think that we must always worship in the future in precisely the same way that our parents and grandparents worshiped. Tradition may actually free us to live in new ways by giving us the perspective of what has worked and what has failed in human history to date.

The celebration period of the two-hour program puts less emphasis on tradition than does the opening service. There is, to be sure, a valuable history of spontaneous worship patterns in the church, which is important to the development of celebration. But the focus of act three is less on the past and more on our attempt to know the living presence of the Spirit. If the emphasis in act one is on providing a grounding for our worship life in tradition, the emphasis in act three shifts to the unknown adventure of the future.

We make a mistake in assuming that most people today can automatically find their way around an experience of traditional worship without some education as to what is involved and why. For many inside the church the familiarity of habit may blind us to the deeper meanings in a traditional service. And for many outside the church the language, the rituals, and the symbolism of church tradition seem out of keeping with modern secular life. The psalmist's plaintive cry is heard from many quarters today: "How shall we sing the Lord's song in a foreign land?" (Psalm 137:4).

The Tradition: Remembering and Responding

An education course in November of 1972 was aimed at trying to help South Church children from grades four to six to understand more of what was happening in act one. The teacher asked each student to share a significant event that had happened to him or her during the past year. The group talked of going to a new school, attending a musical concert, almost being dropped from an ice hockey team, living through an ocean storm, experiencing the death of a grandmother; the teacher mentioned watching the birth of his fourth child. We spent time discussing the importance of *remembering*—of calling to mind important events and sharing them with people about whom we cared.

The class went on to talk about *responding* to what had been remembered. Living through an ocean storm produced the response of fear and excitement; several children tried to act out the feeling they would have had in a storm. We touched on sadness and grief as the response to a grandmother's death; nervousness as the response to going to a new school; anger, and maybe a little guilt, at almost being dropped from a hockey team after a fight on the ice.

The next Sunday the class started out by remembering the significant events that others had shared the week before. We began to recognize that we could remember events that had not happened to us personally but had happened to people who were close to us. And persons could still respond to the memory of events, even if the events did not happen to them personally; we could live into a memory and respond as though the event were ours.

Gradually the class moved to the definition of worship as a time for us to remember and to respond. In a traditional service, people gather to remember significant events in the lives of church people of the past; since those ancient people belong to the same basic community of faith as we do, these people are spiritually close to us in spite of the intervening years. As the church remembers special events in its tradition, we then respond in worship to those memories.

Sometimes congregations have difficulty responding with the vitality and feeling that is appropriate to what they are remembering. How often, for example, do people read the words "Praise the Lord" as though they were reading an arithmetic book? But when these same words are read as though we are remembering an experience of deep joy for people close to us, we may respond in reading with that same joy. The class spent time practicing various responsive readings, litanies, written prayers—attempting to put themselves into what they were saying with a feeling appropriate to the content.

In a small way that class was trying to find the meaning of traditional worship. Act one is a time to remember the total tradition of the people of God. Because we in the church today are a part of that same people of God, our remembering of the tradition is a calling to mind of the life of persons close to us in faith. As we then respond to memory, we allow the tradition to come alive as the roots of Christian worship.

The Old Testament Book of Deuteronomy describes the same process of remembering the significant past as though it had happened to us and of letting that past come alive to shape our religious response:

> When your son asks you in time to come, "What is the meaning of the testimonies and the statutes and the ordinances which the Lord our God has commanded you?" then you shall say to your son, "We were Pharaoh's slaves in Egypt; and the Lord brought us out of Egypt with a mighty hand. . . . And the Lord commanded us to do all these statutes, to fear the Lord our God, for our good always, that he might preserve us alive, as at this day." (Deuteronomy 6:20-21, 24)

A Covenant Renewal Ceremony

The remembering and responding of traditional worship took specific shape on November 18, 1973. Opening worship was designed around the scripture lesson of Joshua 24:1-28. In that story Joshua had gathered all the tribes of Israel at a place called Shechem in Palestine. He asked his people to "choose this day whom you will serve"; either they could serve the Lord, the God of Abraham and Moses, or they could serve the gods of the land in which they had come to live.

The sermon that day tried to sketch out a similar choice for people in this country today. One continuing option is to serve the God of the Bible, who judges all nations and all peoples including our own. A second option is to give allegiance to what has been called a national "civil religion," a powerful faith in this land which has come to identify America as the new chosen people, the nation of righteousness in the midst of a world otherwise dominated by darkness and sin.

The opening service by itself may have succeeded at best in taking a piece of biblical tradition and making it come alive intellectually for some of those present. Joshua lived so long ago that the relevance of his choice at Shechem is hard to grasp; and the idea of a national civil religion is an abstraction that may be equally hard to fathom. Act one may have helped the congregation to remember an important ancient event, but most people's response was little more than curiosity.

The celebration act later that morning, however, provided an opportunity for a much fuller and deeper congregational response. Act three took the same scripture passage from the book of Joshua and used it as the basis for a dramatization here and now of a "covenant renewal ceremony."

The minister opened that celebration by asking all the men of the congregation to come forward—only adult males, not women or children or youth. There were audible expressions of protest! He went on to explain that Joshua's original covenant renewal actually included adult males only. We, however, have no need to be bound today by cultural traditions of people in the Bible who lived three thousand years ago. Modern society has moved beyond Joshua's culture in recognizing that significant religious events should include persons of both sexes and, it is to be hoped, of all ages. The minister then invited everyone present to come forward.

The children in an education class for grades four to six had spent several weeks studying the original biblical Ark of the Covenant and building a cardboard replica, which they then brought into the sanctuary and set on the communion table. The class for children in the first three elementary school grades had pasted their own wording of the Ten Commandments on wooden tablets; that wording included a classic restatement of the seventh: "Do not date others if you are married." These children came forward and placed the wooden tablets inside the ark, just as the biblical ark contained Moses' tablets.

The congregation was invited to join in a procession around the sanctuary, singing and carrying the ark along with us. As we returned to the front, someone took the commandments out of their receptacle and read them one at a time to the people, allowing time for them to affirm their willingness to obey each

"Thou shalt" with an "Amen." Bread and carrot sticks were brought in and served to those present to symbolize the sealing of the covenant.

At the end of the celebration, the minister reminded the congregation that Thanksgiving would be celebrated on the coming Thursday. This holiday is a national covenant renewal ceremony in which the country is called to reaffirm the covenant of thanksgiving which the Pilgrims made with God that first harsh year in New England.

The temptation of Thanksgiving as a national celebration is to make of it a time of worship of a national civil religion. Americans can easily distort that special day into an opportunity to celebrate all the milk and honey, all the abundance and prosperity of this land. The first Thanksgiving, however, was not a time to rejoice in our material wealth; it was an occasion to celebrate the goodness of a God who watches over all people in time of need and who judges each of us according to the way in which we share his bounty with all.

The bread and the carrot sticks of act three could be seen as an appetizer for the main covenant renewal feast which the whole country would be celebrating four days later on Thanksgiving. Could we in that congregation eat the Thanksgiving meal as a seal of a new covenant relationship with the God of the Bible, the God of the Pilgrims? Could this modern parish choose again whom we would serve—just as Joshua's people chose so many centuries ago?

The total experience of worship, education, and celebration provided the opportunity for this congregation to enter into a part of biblical tradition and to let that tradition come alive in our situation today. The remembering and the responding of opening worship were enriched by educational classes and by a celebration reenactment of an ancient drama.

Education and Traditional Worship

In addition to such complex events as a covenant renewal, the education period has been able to provide support and reinforcement for traditional worship in a variety of simpler ways. One class in October of 1972 was entitled "From Shower Singing to Choir Loft." A group of persons whose singing was usually confined to the shower stall—and who might not have had the time to join the regular choir—met for a month to learn an anthem. The final Sunday of that month was planned to include this class as a special choir for opening worship.

New hymns, or old hymns that are good but unfamiliar, can be learned in the education period. On a later Sunday the class that has mastered a particular hymn can serve as a nucleus in worship to help the whole congregation sing it. Act two becomes a means of expanding the parish's musical repertoire.

A children's class could compose a simple prayer to be read aloud during corporate prayer in the opening service—a period of planned silence when individuals may pray silently or out loud as they feel led to do. A small prayer group can meet during education to reinforce the meaning and importance of prayer in worship by carrying the concerns of the congregation to a deeper expression than may be possible in the formal gathering of the whole church.

Many churches have discovered that sermon discussion groups can give added meaning to worship; such groups can meet during the second act of the three-part program. A discussion class geared toward children can help a child begin to understand sermons; it can also give the minister helpful feedback on how he or she can relate at least a part of the sermon to a child's world. As a side value, sermon discussion groups provide an opportunity for the newcomer, the visitor, and the irregular church attender to fit into the whole three-part Sunday morning program without having missed important background in an education course which lasts for several weeks in a row.

The point is that the educational act can be of value in helping people learn how to worship by helping them live into the tradition which informs that worship. When church and church school are parallel and unrelated, this value is lost. But a Sunday morning program which integrates the two allows the church to recover its roots in the tradition in a variety of mutually supportive ways.

Formal Worship

Conventional worship is formal as well as traditional. Worship is a drama. There is a flow and a direction to the drama which allows the congregation to emerge at the end of a service at a different place from where it was at the beginning. This flow or direction is built into the order of the worship pattern and is independent of the particular content of the weekly service within that order.

The broad and varied number of worship patterns which the Christian church has developed in its history suggests that there is no single, standard order or dramatic progression which all services must follow. What is important is that whatever worship order we use be able to lead a congregation into and through a meaningful experience of the gospel.

The particular order which South Church uses in act one starts with an organ prelude, an opening hymn, and what is called "The Preparation": a call to worship, a confession of our humanity in the presence of God, a declaration of God's forgiving grace, an expression of thanksgiving in response to grace. The service moves to a proclamation of the Word of God through scripture and sermon. There follows an opportunity to open ourselves in the light of God's Word to his presence and his will in prayer through the prayers of the minister and of members of the congregation. Act one moves to a climax in the offering of our lives and the fruits of our lives to God's service. A concluding blessing from the minister brings the first period of the three-part service to a close.

People often level the criticism that doing the same thing week after week can become dull, routine, meaningless. There are, however, advantages to a standard order of worship, particularly if the worshipers put themselves into that order with feeling. Congregational familiarity with a pattern of service can lead to a healthy sense of congregational ownership of that order. Worship has less of a tendency to become the minister's or the choir's; the congregation comes to a familiar order with the sense of trust that this is its service.

Modern culture values repetition in many areas. How many television series begin every weekly installment with exactly the same theme song, the same pictures, the same dramatic sequences involving the key actors or actresses? As people hear and see the familiar opening sounds and scenes, they call to mind the memory and the mood of past installments in that same series. Regularly repeated openings give the audience a sense that this is their favorite program: they've seen it before and they know the kind of experience to expect. In the same way the familiar sounds and atmosphere of formal worship call to mind the richness of past church memories and an expectation of the kind of experience people may find again.

Children may on occasion appreciate the value of repetition more than adults. The sermon on Children's Day at South Church in 1972—a sermon with children particularly in mind—used the kind of repetition we often find in campfire storytelling. The Bible lesson that day was Jesus' story of the laborers in the vineyard (Matthew 20:1-16).

The minister started the sermon with a description of a farmer who woke up early one morning and said to himself, "I've got a farm. I've got a big, BIG job. I need some help." (The use of hand gestures gave emphasis to the three simple sentences.) But after a while, the farmer saw that he still had a problem: "I've got a farm. I've got a big, BIG job. I need more help." Again and again the farmer recognized throughout the day that he still had a problem. By the time the minister mentioned the farmer's concern "about the eleventh hour" of the day, the whole congregation was able to join in saying words they now found familiar, in words that were a part of them, too: "I've got a farm. . ."

Familiarity helped that sermon come alive. Repetition, far from making the story dull, routine, dead, created a sense of expectation; the congregation began to look forward to the next time the farmer would see that he had a problem. In the same way the regularity of a standard worship order can be a source of life and expectancy to a church as it gathers week after week.

Content in Formal Worship

A constant order of service can also free people to focus their concern on the content of the experience within that order. If a congregation has come to know where the hymns fit in and when the sermon is given, it may be able to look beyond the order of service to the mood or text of the hymn, to the message of the sermon. A constantly changing order, on the other hand, forces the worshiper to spend considerable energy trying to figure out where she or he is in the service and where that service is going.

The analogy here is to the difference between traveling by car over a familiar and an unfamiliar route. If the route is known, we have little fear of getting lost; we can look at the scenery and appreciate what is happening along the way. When the route is unfamiliar, we do not have the same freedom; most of our attention must focus on signs and landmarks to make sure we are headed in the right direction. Similarly, in a familiar order of worship we know basically where we are going, and we are able as a result to appreciate what happens along the way.

In some ways there is more freedom to express radical or controversial content within a formal worship service than there is in the informal celebration period. Celebration carries with it the possibility that the congregation may be asked to participate in an active way in what is happening. But participation involves risk. The result of that risk is that people may feel inhibited during act three, that they may scale down controversial content in order to keep open the possibility of congregational participation and response. The pressure in celebration is often to stay in safer waters where everyone can touch bottom rather than to move out into the deep which may be over people's heads.

A formal service, however, can treat radical or difficult content precisely because the nature of congregational response is preplanned and -ordered. One may touch on the sensitive and painful problems persons have in trying to cope with death, for example, without putting anyone on the spot who may at that moment be in the midst of grief. Act one may plant a seed whose harvest does not and cannot come for weeks or months.

Each of us needs some sense of security in our worship if we are to be able to enter into issues which touch us at the sensitive core of our lives. The orderliness of a formal service provides that security in the first act of the three part service. In celebration, however, the sense of security in the face of risk can come only from a deepening feeling of trust within the congregation.

Such trust begins and ends with trust in God. But the trust must include a belief that the celebration leader will keep the experience from getting out of hand in an unhealthy way, and a sense that the congregation as a whole will provide a supportive atmosphere within which each person can be himself or herself.

Formal Rituals

The rituals of formal worship allow for the expression of difficult emotion in a way that may not be possible in spontaneous and open-ended sharing. A sermon in June of 1973 treated the story of Elijah and the prophets of Baal at Mount Carmel (1 Kings 18:20-39). Elijah set up a contest between himself and the prophets of Baal to see whose god was able to bring fire to a sacrificial offering in response to prayer.

At one point in the sermon the congregation was asked to play the role of the prophets of Baal and to chant the ritual "O Baal, answer us." As the chant developed momentum the minister took on the role of Elijah and taunted the prophets of Baal: "Cry aloud, for he is a god; either he is musing, or he has gone aside, or he is on a journey, or perhaps he is asleep and must be awakened" (1 Kings 18:27).

As the chant became louder, the mocking became more

intense. People found themselves caught up in the expression of feelings that are often too difficult or too painful to share openly in public: anger, exasperation. Baal, of course, did not answer the chanting prayers, and the model sacrifice remained untouched. But Elijah's God did respond for "the eyes of faith" to prayer by "consuming" the offering (in the sermon Elijah's offering was imaginary from the beginning, thus making it easy for the table to be empty after the offering was "consumed").

"And when all the people saw it, they fell on their faces; and they said, 'The Lord, he is God; the Lord, he is God' " (18:39). Here was a new ritual to chant. Slowly the anger subsided as people poured themselves into a formalized expression of faith: "The Lord, he is God."

The whole experience above took place within a sermon. The response of the congregation was ordered; the words were planned in advance. The hymns, the prayers, the offering of that whole service helped to place the sermon in perspective. Yet people's sense of the structure of that formal worship allowed them the freedom to put themselves into the chanting of rituals with a feeling they might have hesitated to express on their own.

Our anger, our exasperation today is not over the failure of a Middle Eastern god to burn an animal sacrifice. But we have our own experiences of anger and frustration which open our ability to empathize with Elijah and the prophets of Baal; and that empathy may give us the perspective of history on the feelings that capture us. The final affirmation of faith by Elijah's people can still be a channel to receive and to shape the human emotions we know today so that they become most constructive.

Family Worship—Pluralistic Age Levels

One of the more difficult aspects of the opening worship at South Church is the attempt to include children. There is, to be sure, a nursery for the youngest children and for a few individuals in the earliest elementary school grades who may find it particularly difficult to sit through a formal service every week. But the church does make an effort to involve children as young as the first grade in the first act of the Sunday morning drama.

Our understanding of family worship is that different portions of a service should be aimed at different age groups. We are not looking for an experience which focuses throughout on the lowest common age-denominator. Some portions of act one are designed explicitly to meet adults at an adult level. Other portions are designed to include children. And the elements which involve children are spread throughout the service.

Many families in their homes try to plan dinner conversations when everybody gathers together so that each age level has its turn. The youngest children can claim a share of the family's attention to tell about their day and can expect brothers and sisters and parents to listen. Teen-agers have their turn. And the parents may also stake out a block of time to catch up with each other at an adult level: "Mommy and Daddy haven't seen each other all day, and we need to talk to each other for a few minutes. Please wait quietly while we talk. We'll listen to you in a minute."

What is happening in this simple example of dinner conversation is that a family is trying to define a life-style of pluralistic age levels. No one tries to tie the family to any one age level—either to say that all conversation must take place at the child's level of understanding or to say that all conversation must be adult and children should be "seen and not heard." Everyone has a chance; no single age level dominates.

South Church has tried to pattern family worship along similar lines. Opening worship attempts to reflect a concern for pluralistic age levels. Some of the service is planned so that children can understand and participate. Yet some of the experience is designed openly as "Mommy and Daddy time" for parents and older people to grapple with the issues of faith and life at an adult level.

Once a congregation recognizes that family worship can mean a service of pluralistic age levels, it can plan accordingly.

There is no need to try to make children listen to the whole sermon, but there is a need to ask children to be quiet enough to allow adults to listen. And the older members of the parish need to respect the fact that children are an important part of the church family, too.

We have tried to make pencils and paper available in the pews. These are partly for adults who wish to make notes or jot down messages for the minister or the deacons. But paper and pencil are also important for children. A young child can draw pictures during a formal service without disturbing others who are caught up in listening to what is being said or sung.

If the congregation makes a conscious decision to welcome children who may draw during worship, it is providing an important atmosphere. At the practical level it will take the time to make sure that paper and pencils are available. But in a deeper way the parish can communicate to children an important sense of belonging to the community of faith. Young and old can be themselves, yet together they can still be part of a common church family.

Children in Act One

A formal order of worship does provide a number of places where children can participate. Many parishes have developed children's and junior choirs, which sing anthems that reflect the preferences of a variety of age groups. Education classes can teach some of the great hymns of the church so that young people can feel at home in singing these in worship. Children and youth are often excited by being asked to usher and to collect the morning offering. They can also help (as is already being done in many churches) in lighting candles as the service begins.

The opportunities for children in formal litanies have barely been touched by most of us in the church; classes on dramatic reading can bring children to feel what is happening even if an intellectual understanding of every word is not yet a possibility. A church could design a simple litany for its Sunday morning worship which could also be used by families in their religious life at home—for prayers at bedtime or a grace at meals. And when church litanies are used in the home, an important connection is made between the church and the rest of our lives in the world.

If a conventional service provides an opportunity for children to participate, it also carries the risk that adults may turn their children into spectacles for people to watch. How many times have children's choirs been paraded in front of the congregation, not to lead the church in its worship, but rather to give parents an excuse to embarrass their children for the sake of parental pride? Children need to be treated as persons with their own needs and hopes just as adults do.

Even the Sunday sermon can include children. When the main focus of the sermon is the adults in the congregation, it is still possible to spend some of the sermon time dealing with the message of the morning at a child's level.

This parish has tried on occasion to work out what might be called "concentric circle" preaching: the first part of the sermon is aimed at children; the second part is focused at a youth level; and the concluding part of the sermon is given at an adult level. While preaching is aimed at the youngest age group, it can still speak to the whole circle of the congregation, as youth and adults can obviously understand what is being said. As the focus shifts to an older age group, however, the circle of people who can follow the message becomes smaller and smaller.

One concentric circle sermon was entitled "The Parable of the Porcupine." The minister started out by trying to tame an imaginary porcupine by stroking it, with the painful result that he got some imaginary quills "stuck" in his hand. Children were involved in this part of the sermon—so much so that a few came up to "play" with the imaginary porcupine at the end of the service.

But as the sermon progressed, the minister moved to a deeper level and talked about the reasons why porcupines have quills: porcupines do not believe that people or other animals have their best interests at heart. The quills are protection against being hurt or killed. At the end we were looking at the way each one of us is a human porcupine with our own "quills" sticking out because of our lack of trust in other people around us. God's attempt to tame us in Christ led to the "quills" of suffering and death on the Cross. The whole sermon was structured, in effect, to include the children's sermon as the introduction and the adult's sermon as the conclusion.

Obviously, too, the presence of acts two and three within the total Sunday morning program is a help in the task of involving children. Education classes can be much more active than formal worship. The child who has to struggle to sit through worship, even a shortened forty-five-minute service, can look forward to a class where he or she can move around and do many more things without the ordered discipline of act one.

Celebration too allows much more freedom and opportunity for a child's self-expression. Act three is another experience in the church sanctuary, another experience of worship, but the connotations of that experience to a child are quite different from the connotations of a conventional service. There is, in short, enough variety in the three acts of the Sunday morning service to enable imaginative leaders to involve children throughout.

Why Family Worship?

When we finish the most skillful planning of formal worship for pluralistic age levels, we still find such worship to be difficult. Good family worship is simply hard to do. What is important finally is why a church wants to provide a formal service for all ages. If the reasons are superficial or inadequate, the difficulties may well win out and the parish may gradually "weed out" the children and the youth from its worship. If the reasons are important, however, the congregation will look for ways to live with or to overcome difficulties for the sake of a higher goal.

To me, family worship in church is an important support and reinforcement for the life of the family in the modern world. So much of life today leads a family on separate paths—the adults in one world, the children in another, the youth in a third. Even in church, where we talk about the importance of the family at length, we usually end up acting out a separateness in the way we carry on our discussions: adults talk in one room, and children and youth go to their separate rooms. What kind of image do we project when church school and church are isolated and unrelated institutions, one for the young and the other for the old?

Granted, it is enormously difficult to worship as a family in church. It is also enormously difficult to live as a family in the world. A life-style of pluralistic age levels in the church may be one important way to learn through experience what it means to be a family in today's complex society. For some people, the primary experience of family life is at home with parents and children; for others, such as widows or single persons, what is primary may be the family of the church. But however people know it, a solid family life can be crucial as they face the loneliness, alienation, and anxiety of the modern world.

An integrated Sunday morning program of worship, education, and celebration for all ages is one attempt to support the life of the family by bringing different age groups together in a variety of experiences. There is no requirement here that different ages always be together in the same room; education classes often separate people into rough age groupings in the belief that we learn better sometimes with people our own age. When the separateness becomes institutionalized, however, and the young and the old no longer feel at home with each other in important areas of church life, then we have lost vital richness and depth in what it means to be a community of faith.

Summary

The opening worship period of the three-part Sunday morning program is an important part, though not the only important part, of the life of the church. Act one gives more emphasis to order than to spirit, though there is room for the life of the Spirit within its order. Worship is traditional in that it brings to bear the richness of the tradition of the church on people's experience of the presence of God. A formal service frees the congregation to begin moving beneath its familiar structure of worship to the content of the worship experience. And finally, the church's worship can support a significant image of family life by allowing room for pluralistic age levels within the order of service.

Worship is both an act with completeness and integrity in itself and an act which can introduce the larger drama of worship, education, and celebration. It is to the second act of that drama that we now turn our attention.

3
Education

It can be useful to distinguish two different kinds of religious education: the teaching about religion, and the teaching of religion. Each of these is important. It is not possible to draw a fine line between them, there being unavoidable overlap. Yet it is the second, I believe, the broad area of the teaching of religion, which should be the primary focus of an educational program in the church.

The teaching *about* religion is the objective presentation of religion as a part of the total body of human knowledge which humankind has accumulated over the course of the centuries and which believer and nonbeliever alike should know as a part of being educated. Such teaching about religion is both legal and appropriate as a subject within the public schools. It is this kind of religious education to which Mr. Justice Clark referred in the 1963 United States Supreme Court prayer and Bible-reading decision *(Abington School District v. Schempp):*

> In addition, it might well be said that one's education is not complete without a study of comparative religion or the history of religion and its relationship to the advancement of civilization. It certainly may be said that the Bible is worthy of study for its literary and historic qualities. Nothing we have said here indicates that such

study of the Bible or of religion, when presented objectively as part of a secular program of education, may not be effected consistent with the First Amendment.[1]

The teaching *of* religion, on the other hand, involves the ways in which the religious community passes on its own way of life—its history, beliefs, rituals, and traditions—to potential believers or to actual believers who wish to deepen their participation in that way of life. In a variety of church-state decisions, the Supreme Court has held that the teaching of religion within public education is unconstitutional in this country.

There is no implication in the above definitions that public education has been successful in fulfilling its responsibilities in the teaching about religion. Some progress has been made, and I would hope that the public schools may grow in this area. What can be said on the other side, however, is that probably no institution in society—at least not state-supported education—can be counted on to take any major responsibility for the teaching *of* religion if the church neglects the task. Passing on a religious way of life in the hope that people will participate in it is a crucial educational need in and for the church; and the church may be the only group that can meet that need.

This definition of the teaching of religion is not simply a statement of what the church ought to be doing in its religious education program. It is also a descriptive statement of what the church is actually doing. Whether one likes it or not, the community of faith does have a particular way of life already and is involved in passing on that way, the good and the bad. Day-to-day parish life unavoidably communicates both the humanity and the divine promise of the church (all too often the former far more than the latter) to those who share and hear of that life.

What becomes important, then, is thinking through how the church's way of life can be recognized, articulated, and shared in such a way that people can be led into a deeper participation. What is also important is the continuing need to examine, judge, and seek to redeem that life in the light of Jesus Christ, so that persons of all ages can be led through involvement in the church to a deeper participation in him.

When church education is seen as the passing on of a way of life rather than the objective presentation of accumulated knowledge, one gains an important perspective on the organizational problems of religious education in a parish. Specifically, when church school is separate from church, it becomes difficult to pass on the church's way of life in that school. How can one institution, the Sunday school, deepen an individual's sense of belonging and participation in another institution, the church, if the two are basically parallel and unrelated?

Religious education as the sharing of the church's way of life is far more compatible with an integrated church and church school. The education program can then help the congregation to reflect on its total way of life from the vantage point of standing within that way. Individuals involved in the process of religious education can continue to learn at the same time that they become more deeply involved in the life of the parish.

A child may need to experience a personal belonging to a community of faith before he or she can feel the purpose and meaning of celebrating Holy Communion with that community. Again, teaching personal morality outside the context of mutual participation in a community of faith is often seen as preaching at someone; while the teaching of personal morality within a caring church family can become a means of supporting each other. Few today will pay any attention to the former, but few are unwilling to recognize the importance of the latter in this world of loneliness, alienation, dehumanization.

As stated earlier, one cannot draw a neat line between the teaching about religion and the teaching of religion. Obviously the latter includes some factual presentations which should be as objective as possible. The difference between the two kinds of religious education, however, is basically in whether one learns about religion from the outside or the inside. Surely there is room for some of both. But the particular role of the church, I believe, should be the latter, the teaching of religion from the inside.

The three-part Sunday morning service at South Church includes a program of religious education as the second or middle act. That program has come to give more emphasis to the teaching of religion than to the teaching about religion. In one sense all three acts of worship, education, and celebration involve the teaching of religion, since all three are ways by which the religious community passes on its way of life—its history, beliefs, rituals, and traditions. Yet act two is particularly important in bringing into focus the learning dimension of our full two hours together.

Examples of the Teaching of Religion

A good example of what is meant by the teaching of religion is the confirmation class at South Church. It was no longer possible within the three-part Sunday morning program to think of confirmation as the point of graduation from Sunday school into church. The youth who came to a membership class in act two already felt themselves to be a part of the church family through their involvement in the total program of worship, education, and celebration. Confirmation for them was neither the end of church school nor the beginning of church.

Participants in the class were asked instead to confirm their ongoing feeling of belonging to the church. The course focused on an examination of the nature of the church in which they were already involved—comparing the biblical promise with the reality experienced in this congregation. No one tried to hide the obvious defects, or the good points.

At the end of the course, each person was asked to decide whether or not to accept personal responsibility to help the church conform to its promise and to join in the congregation's efforts to serve in Christ's mission to the world. The whole process of confirmation was an attempt to understand the church from the inside. And the final confirmation service was designed as an opportunity for each confirmand who wished to do so to give public witness in worship that he or she accepted being on the inside of the church, with all the responsibilities this entailed.

Another example of the teaching of religion was a class in March of 1972 entitled "A Christian Welcome." Class members worked on a wooden cradle to give to newborn children in the parish. With considerable help from individuals outside the Sunday morning education period, the group cut, glued, sanded, and finished a rocking cradle, twenty-one and a half inches long. The course members also sewed blankets, sheets, pillow covers, and a mattress cover to fit inside.

Ever since that class, a church member has taken the "South Church cradle" to a family as soon as a baby is born into the family. The new parents are told that the cradle is a prebaptismal gift, expressing the love of God and his church for them at this special time. The cradle is long enough to hold a baby for a few weeks; when the cradle is outgrown, the parents are asked to bring it back so that it can be ready for the next baby.

Making that cradle was an attempt to express the church's belief that the birth of a child is a gift of God to be celebrated. A group of persons with hammer and sandpaper, needle and thread, became involved in one form of Christian education, in learning how to express caring for other people at important times in their lives. Now, every time the cradle is brought into a new home, the church's way of life is passed on through beautiful wood and cloth.

The teaching of religion also touches on questions of parish business. Act two has been used as a vehicle to improve communication within the organizational life of the congregation. A favorite course is the periodic "Church Council Corner" where anyone can share personal concerns about the parish with those who have the responsibility of decision-making in between full congregational meetings. Another well-attended class has been the training sessions for persons willing to serve in the every member canvass, the fund drive for the church's operating budget.

Both a church council corner and a pledge drive training course are specific ways by which a congregation passes on its particular way of life. By dealing with parish business in the education period, we have been able to bring a religious education dimension to those issues; fund drive training, for example, provided the opportunity to discuss deeper issues in the theology of stewardship and tithing. We have also found that some people whose primary concern is related to organizational questions have been drawn through those questions into the church's education program.

Education After Worship

The education period at South Church takes place immediately after the conclusion of opening worship. Act one is the background and the foundation for what happens in act two. And the education courses can be designed to tie in directly to the opening service.

The idea of an opening service of worship to be followed by education classes is familiar in a different form to many Sunday schools. These schools often gather all the classes for a brief opening service before the different age groups disperse to individual classrooms. The three-part Sunday morning program simply relieves the church school of responsibility for this opening worship by starting the morning with the whole church's regular formal worship. In this way the entire time of act two can be spent on religious education.

The relationship of education courses to opening worship can be seen in the events of September of 1973 at South Church, a period of time planned around the theme of "creation month." The minister gave a series of sermons on the doctrine of creation; the music for the opening service was planned to fit that same theme. Then in act two various courses met to examine different aspects of creation at different age levels.

The youngest elementary school children were invited to bring into class such things as beetles, butterflies, gerbils, flowers, vegetables, weeds, or any other insects or small animals or plants they might find. Anyone who could find a magnifying glass was asked to bring that in, too. The class also read the account in the first chapter of Genesis of God's creation of plants and animals.

A group of older elementary school children met in a class entitled "A Master Plan for the World." They examined God's plan in creation at the beginning of the book of Genesis. The children then studied the basic idea of ecology and tried to see how human beings are upsetting God's plan by waste and pollution.

During the celebration periods that month, these classes (and others) shared what they were learning with the rest of the congregation. Out of that sharing came questions and concerns for future sermons on creation. When children could see a connection between their Sunday school class and a part of what the minister was saying from the pulpit, both worship and education took on deeper meaning. And the final celebration that September, the climax of the month, was an all-church picnic and a "creation scavenger hunt" in the out-of-doors.

Some education courses may relate in a larger way to the overall meaning of worship. In 1974 an adult class for Lent was planned as a study of Holy Communion. In the church's monthly education mailing to the parish one could read the following course description:

> *A Study of Communion.* We celebrate Communion once a month, but many of us find it difficult to penetrate below words and rituals to the meaning of that ancient and special Christian worship experience. Paul's First Letter to the Corinthians (Chapter 11, verses 17-34) provides a Biblical background for our study, but we need to set that background against the questions of what "broken body" and "new life" mean to us today. We have been using a particular Communion Service in South Church for the past three years; but we may have questions about what that service means and why we do things the way we do. Are there possibilities for making our celebration of Communion more meaningful—if so, we may pass on suggestions to the Board of Deacons for their consideration.

Eventually the class did come up with several minor recommendations which were brought to the Board of Deacons and finally adopted. But the discussion which led to those recommendations may have been more valuable than any specific changes proposed. Coming out of a particular experience of worship, class members were able to reflect back on what worship meant to them. But the small group in that course was also able to enter into detailed study of the Bible passages which shape one kind of worship, the Communion service. In between the fresh experience of God's presence and the study of the biblical record, the class tried to wrestle with what happens when the bread is broken and the cup is shared.

Individuals who wanted to learn more about the Eucharist had the opportunity in that course to do so. And persons who had suggestions for deepening that experience were able to gain a hearing for their ideas. Finally, as each participant shared with the group what was important to him or her in the Lord's Supper, all of us found our understanding of the Communion service to be broadened and enriched.

Education Before Celebration

Not only does the South Church education program take place after formal worship; it also occurs immediately before the informal worship experience of celebration. The opportunity for the entire congregation to gather for a third act after education can give a sense of purpose and direction to the classes of act two.

Much of the content of celebration grows out of the education courses. The final act of the three-part service is often a time when classes can share parts of their experience with a larger group, which can then appreciate that experience, ask questions to draw out its meaning, and give focus to what is happening. By the same token, advance knowledge that there is a celebration period after act two helps to shape the planning of the content in the education program.

The parish mailing for October of 1972 included the following course description:

> *UNICEF Month*—for Grades 3-6. It's the month for trick and treat. Let's find out about some of the children in other countries with whom we share when we fill those orange and black boxes. Each Sunday will be a singing, dancing, speaking, cooking and "making something" experience—with shared leadership.

The celebration period on October 29 was planned ahead of time as "A Lunch for the Hungry"—the kind of meal that our UNICEF Halloween gifts provide for starving people around the world. The congregation was asked to read the biblical story of the Last Judgment in Matthew 25:31-46 as preparation, and then was invited to gather around the communion table.

The UNICEF class had cooked a large pot of lentils and rice during the education period that Sunday. Members had also mixed up a batch of powdered milk. This food was now brought into the sanctuary and set on the specially covered communion table. Everyone was invited to come forward and eat the actual meal which Halloween pennies make possible around the world.

There was little need that Sunday for a lot of words to tell the congregation what was happening to them in that celebration. By eating that simple meal, people found a deeper empathy for those whose hunger would be met by such food. As we shared around the Lord's Table, we were attempting to celebrate the presence of Christ, who said, "For I was hungry and you gave me food, I was thirsty and you gave me drink, I was a stranger and you welcomed me" (Matthew 25:35).

The effect of celebration on the education period was also apparent on November 25, 1973. The three-, four-, and five-year-olds had been studying various important men and women in the Old Testament. That particular Sunday they had looked at Joshua and had learned the familiar spiritual, "The Battle of Jericho." These children came into the sanctuary for act three carrying a number of wooden blocks from the toy chest.

As the congregation gathered for celebration, the minister asked people how many of them had a secret desire to tear down a wall. About two-thirds of those present raised their hands. He went on to invite those who wanted to join in to gather in a circle around the communion table. Most of those who had raised their hands a moment before joined the circle—homemakers, children, a college administrator, a businessman, and a variety of others.

The children then built a simple wall out of the blocks they had brought in with them. Once again the communion table (this time covered with a heavy felt cloth) served as the focus of the celebration as the children built their wall on it. The circle of people then walked around the table singing, "Joshua fought the battle of Jericho." After the group had marched and sung for a couple of minutes, the piano stopped playing and the children ran spontaneously, without cue, into the center to knock the wall of blocks down.

No one tried on that Sunday, either, to take a lot of words to interpret what people were doing. There was no attempt to moralize—if, indeed, it is even possible to moralize about Joshua's conquest of Jericho in the sixth chapter of the book of Joshua. Yet the simple acting out of that biblical story with young and old participating together helped to make it come alive for each one of us.

The Effect on Education of Being In-Between

As the second act in the three-part program, education courses take place in between the opening worship service and the closing celebration. The time available for church school classes is therefore limited at both ends. If act one runs longer than planned, the second act can be squeezed. And if members of the congregation linger after worship for long conversations with each other, the education period can be squeezed even further.

Perhaps the most frequently heard criticism of the three-part program since its inception is the complaint that there is not enough time for religious education. When the two-hour program is working at its smoothest, it allows some forty-five minutes for classes in act two. But given human limitations, these classes are often unable to count on the full three-quarters of an hour.

It is, of course, a possibility to discipline the congregation to move quickly from worship to classes in act two. Yet many people react against too much pressure in this direction. Modern life can be hurried and hectic enough during the rest of the week without people having to feel that a stopwatch is being held on their experience of God in church on Sunday.

The best congregational discipline for getting swiftly to act two seems to come from the content of education courses and not from the hands of a clock. When people look forward to a particular class, they tend to get to that class relatively soon after the opening service. And obviously, if the education period is filled with interesting content, people will have more time to learn that content.

On given individual occasions it is always possible for a class to continue right through, and even (if necessary) beyond, the celebration period. No law forces people to come back to the sanctuary for act three. If a class is caught up in a topic or project of particular importance, it may be far better for it to skip celebration on that Sunday.

When the three-part program was new at South Church, we spent much more time than we do now in encouraging people to return to the sanctuary for the last act. Nobody really knew what celebration was all about, and without some congregational responsibility to develop act three, the whole two-hour program would have suffered. As celebration has built up its own history, however, it has begun to stand on its own feet. The church has found much less need to treat that period as a responsibility. From a backlog of experience, the congregation has begun to know what to expect in that last act. Those who want to come, do, and those who don't, stay away; enough continue to come to make celebration worthwhile.

The education period still faces a definite limit at the end. Most classes try to finish by 11:40, and it is a rare one which continues through till noon. Act two has become limited, however, not so much by explicit congregational pressure for people to come to celebration as by growing congregational expectation of the kinds of things that can happen there.

There is another side of the coin to the problem of limited time for act two. Coming out of our particular history at South Church, the three-part program did cut down the amount of time available for children's religious education, but it also opened up a whole new program of adult education. The price we paid was a shorter period of time for individual classes, but the goal we achieved was a program involving all ages in Christian education.

The limited education time has also led the church to offer courses which last several months. At the initial stages of the development of the two-hour program, most courses ran for only a month at a time. But people's interests and desires have grown since then. Adult courses, in particular, have come to last for several months in order to allow greater depth of treatment for some topics. A class on the meaning of death, for example, might well continue for three months, or even four.

Again, there is no reason why the entire program of parish religious education must take place on Sunday morning. If class time is too short in the three-part program, the congregation can always schedule additional hours at another time during the week, especially during Advent or Lent.

Perhaps the most telling advantage, in the long run, to placing church school in between worship and celebration is the opportunity to integrate the religious education program of the parish into the rest of parish life. Learning is no longer something that occurs in a separate compartment unrelated to the central worship experiences of the church. It becomes possible to understand religious education as a dimension of all three acts of the Sunday morning program.

It is instructive to look at the developing organizational responsibilities for the three-part program at South Church. When the three-part service was initiated, the Board of Education in the parish had responsibility for act two, and the Board of Deacons had responsibility for the two worship experiences in acts one and three. In time, as we understood the immense educational possibilities in the celebration period, the congregation decided to give joint responsibility for act three to the deacons and the Board of Education. More recently the Board of Education has tried to open a dialogue with the deacons about the educational possibilities and implications of the opening worship service in act one.

What is happening, in effect, is that two boards are beginning to see that they have joint responsibility for each act in the three-part service. It is unrealistic to think that worship stops at the end of act one and that religious education does not begin until the opening of act two. What seems far more natural is the idea that there is a worship dimension and an educational dimension to each of the three different experiences of the two-hour program. In that sense, instead of seeing the three-part service as a program which reduces the time for education, one can see such a service in the opposite light: when South Church moved from a program of simultaneous church and church school to a two-hour service in three acts, it really expanded the time for Christian education from one hour to two hours.

Scheduling religious education in between worship and celebration opens the door to a healthy process of creative interaction. The quality and the content of each act can be stimulated by the others. The only boundary line to the possibilities of that open door seems to be the horizon of imagination in the people of the church.

The Content of Act Two

One of the best words to describe the specific content of the education period in the three-act program of South Church is the term *eclectic*. We have borrowed from whatever appears to work, often adapting material as we use it to the needs of this congregation and the new possibilities of the two-hour service.

Teachers have used various curricular resources from a number of different denominations. Other courses have been homemade. At one point a couple of years ago, the Board of Education analyzed the church's membership list from the perspective of each person's talents, job, or personal interests, which led to the development of a packet of 170 course and teacher possibilities in the parish. That packet has helped to stimulate course ideas ever since.

Besides being eclectic, the education courses offered in act two can be grouped in two categories: religious topics and personal relationships. Having a variety of classes from these two areas does help to hold the interest of a diverse congregation and to attract people to the whole three-part program.

One of the interesting trends of the last few years at South Church has been a gradual recovery of interest in traditional religious topics for the education program. In years past the Sunday school in this parish had had its share of such topics. But in the fall of 1970 the congregation moved out in a different direction with the interest-oriented progressive education of the experimental church school. Instead of beginning with age-old religious topics and attempting to make these interesting, the experimental program turned the process around; courses were planned around people's interests, and the attempt was made to relate those interests to religious faith.

With the development of the Sunday morning program of worship, education, and celebration, much of the creativity and research which led into the experimental church school found its way into celebration. As a result, the education period was able to recover some of the value in the older concern for traditional religious issues. As innovation flowed into act three, the second act was able to settle back into a more lasting balance between the new and the old.

The 1970 experimental religious education program had highlighted a number of principles: the variety of content which is appropriate for consideration; the desire to build on the interests of people, young and old; the involvement of persons in an active way in what is happening; the importance of self-expression and the sharing of faith; the cultivation of a spirit of adventure and a willingness to take risks. Most important of all may have been the concern for bringing individuals of different ages together in a mutually supportive experience. All these principles have come to influence the celebration period of the three-act program.

As celebration has grown, the education program has become less controversial and more open to the variety of needs and hopes in a diverse parish. There is no inherent reason why every course must begin with the Bible; nor is there any reason why every class must start where the participants' interests lie. Some persons prefer the former, and others the latter. And the chances are that both kinds of people can be found in any given congregation.

Then too, the three-part program has had an important effect on the critical area of politics within the church. In 1970 the Board of Education in the parish was dominated by a strong group of people who were understood to be "liberals." Church school was seen as a program at one extreme end of the pendulum swing. Those who saw themselves as "conservatives" felt left out; at one time a group even attempted to overthrow the experimental program and institute a conservative evangelical curriculum in its place. Given the constituency of South Church, such a curriculum would have been as far out on the other end of the pendulum swing as the experimental program was on its end.

It has been a major change to move from those struggles and pendulum swings to the present eclectic content of the education program in the three-part service. Instead of moving back and forth from one extreme to the other in its content, act two has settled into a healthy tension between courses that emphasize religious topics and those that focus on personal relationships. No course is perfect, and nobody has all the problems of religious education solved. Reconciliation in the parish was achieved when "liberals" and "conservatives" decided there was room for the insights of both. That reconciliation has been solidified as people have gradually recognized that labels such as "liberal" and "conservative" do not adequately describe the richness and complexity of any human being.

Courses on Religious Topics

Most of the courses in act two probably fall in the more traditional area of religious topics. This is definitely true for courses during the major religious season of Lent. But it may well be true for the total education program, too, reflecting the particular composition of South Church at this point in its history.

Children in grades one to three have studied such Old Testament figures as King Saul and King David. In addition to some biblical work, the class members experimented with how it feels to be king and how it feels to be ruled by a king. The class then prepared a short skit out of their experiments, which they put on for the rest of the church in a celebration period.

Another month these same children studied New Testament stories and made a diorama of Jesus and the money-changers in the Temple to be displayed on the communion table in act three. The older elementary children have worked with New Testament parables; a simple reenactment of the story of the prodigal son during act three one Sunday helped this parable come alive.

Adult courses have ranged from a study of women in the Bible to a listening study of death and resurrection themes in music. One class spent several months learning about the early church, with a special section on Good Friday and Easter in that church. Act two has provided the opportunity to treat such ethical issues as public housing in this community and political issues in the 1972 national election in the light of our Christian responsibilities.

Modern religious figures such as Martin Luther King, Jr., and Daniel Berrigan have served as the focus for popular adult study courses. Other topics include faith and healing, prophecy and fulfillment, an experience of prayer, anthropology and biblical faith, and a spiritual life-style. When appropriate, insights from classes such as these have been shared with the whole congregation in the celebration period; and the insights have on occasion led people to put their faith to work in new ways.

Courses for youth have treated such broadly religious topics as "Life or Death?—Who Decides," "Justice for Juveniles," and "Who Is This Man Jesus?" Young people have used the second act to plan a weekend retreat and to finish working on a future Youth Sunday service of worship. Oftentimes, various high school students have joined adult classes.

A number of parishes in recent years have found the value of making religious banners. A variety of age groups have participated in this activity at South Church, too. As people sew, they can learn the particular message of the banner. Act three opens up a host of possibilities for these banners: every member of the congregation can take a single stitch during celebration so as to feel a part of the final product; the banners can be consecrated or dedicated; and act three can be enriched by these colorful messages carried in an occasional procession around the sanctuary.

Courses Focusing on Personal Relationships

The faith content of a religious-topics course on Christian symbols may be obvious. But in classes whose primary motivation is the deepening of personal relationships, the faith content may be harder to recognize. The chairperson of one of the church boards and a first-year member of the children's choir may not see any immediate religious education in working together in their old clothes to paint a wall, but they may discover when they have finished that passing the Peace of Christ to each other means much more than it did before they started.

There is no value in trying to make a hard-and-fast distinction between religious-topics courses in one compartment and personal-relationships courses in another. Most classes involve some of both emphases. The point is rather that some courses are more concerned about what is under discussion or what is being created than they are about the relationships which develop between class members; and other courses place their emphasis the other way around.

In May of 1973 South Church offered a course entitled "Beginning a Braided Rug." The course description read as follows:

> A braided rug would add just the right touch to the reading area in the library, especially if many folks had a part in making it. Let's take the first step. Bring a pair of scissors and a woolen garment which you would like to live on as part of this rug (lightweight wool is best—from a dress, skirt, pair of slacks). We will cut the garments into strips as the beginning of our braided rug.

As the course evolved, it was led by two members of an elderly women's sewing group in the church. Some members of that group had become involved in parts of the three-act program, mostly in coming to the opening worship service; but other members still remained hesitant about "all the changes" in the church.

The importance of the braided rug project lay not so much in any religious content as in the fact that it became a vehicle through which an important group of people in the church family could enter into new areas of the Sunday morning program. When the rug was finally finished and consecrated in celebration, one of the women in the sewing group was ecstatic. This was her first celebration experience. She could hardly wait to go back and tell the other members of the group what act three was like: "This is really great!"

As another example, a Vietnam veteran led a class in January of 1973 on what it was like to be in that war in Southeast Asia. The content of the course was important, but far more important was the opportunity for him to share intensely painful experiences within a supportive community. He knew that these memories had to be integrated into a life of faith in some way if that faith was to remain relevant. The support of other people was what he needed.

Again, in September of 1973, a retired farmer in the congregation used an education class to share his love of the land and the soil with the children of the parish (most of whom knew only town or city life). The content of farming was significant—though not necessarily religious—but what became far more meaningful was the friendship which developed between the farmer, a deacon in the church, and the children.

Finally, in October and November of 1973, two high school students led a class in candlemaking. Eventually the class created the candles which were used in the congregation's Advent wreath and candle ceremonies. But the two-month course was also important for developing personal relationships. Youth had an opportunity to teach, and adults were able to learn from them; this reversing of the usual roles helped the participants to get to know each other in new ways.

Involving People in the Process of Learning

This chapter opened with a discussion of the teaching of religion. A church's religious education program might equally well be described as the learning of religion. Those who have been involved in planning act two have consistently urged that courses try to enlist an active participation by all ages in the process of learning.

In the spring of 1974 the preschool children were learning some of the parables of Jesus. One Sunday they studied the invitation to the banquet (or marriage feast) in Matthew 22:1-10. The teacher had prepared some food ahead of time, and act two involved the class members in setting the table and blowing up balloons for a party. When everything was ready, the children invited the toddlers from the next room in to share in their banquet.

As a final touch, the leftover food was brought down to the sanctuary for the celebration period. During that final act the preschoolers came forward and laid out a place setting of silverware on the communion table. They then invited the whole congregation to share in their party. As the minister read the parable from Matthew, the children passed trays of food to all who were present.

During an earlier fall, grade school children spent several Sundays actively involved in learning about God's creation. These children tramped through the woods and fields one Sunday collecting materials to use in making dyes. The following Sunday those materials were brought in and boiled in the church kitchen. The leader for the class had sewed strips of material out of plain cloth in advance of the course; the children were able with careful assistance to dip those strips into the natural dyes. The climax of that education class came when members walked proudly into a celebration period to present the minister with a new pokeberry and onion stole.

The first major breakthrough for youth involvement in the three-part Sunday morning program illustrates again the importance of participation by the learner in the process of education. In May of 1972 a class for young people entitled "The Get Togethers" was offered. Instead of a course taught to youth by adults, this offering was described as "a group for people who like to sing songs about war, poverty, etc.—protest songs and others. If you have a guitar or drums, please bring them." Some of these songs were done again in act three.

Adult involvement in the learning process has usually been through either music or discussion. A three-month course in the winter of 1973 combined elements of both. "Black History and Religion" was a class "looking at Black History in America both prior to the Civil War and after the Civil War up through the recent protest movements." Included in the course description was the statement "We will look at Black music from various periods of that history as a means of understanding history."

The three-month course was appreciated by many adults in South Church because of its depth and quality. It is a good example of the kind of adult education possible during act two.

Portions of the course descriptions for the second and third months are reproduced below:

> This month we will look at American religiosity as seen in slave religion and the spirituals. We will try to understand the uniqueness of the religion of black folks in America, how these people not only reacted to the Christianity presented to them but also created something new. . . . During this concluding month we will consider Reconstruction (after the Civil War) and the legal basis of civil rights, the development of segregation and of civil rights movements in the 20th century. The final session in March will look ahead to May, and ways in which, after Easter, South Church might learn about, and even do something about, pressing problems in our own community.

One final example of enlisting people's participation in the educational process is a course offered to all ages in January of 1973. The course was entitled "Parable Charades." As it turned out, the persons who came to the class on the first Sunday it was offered were all adults. With this age group the participants simply acted out a parable for the rest of the class, and those who watched tried to guess which parable it was.

On the following Sunday the persons who came to "Parable Charades" were all elementary school children. The rules of the game had to be changed, since few children knew enough parables to be able to guess what was being acted out. Instead we all took a common parable and read it from the New Testament. Then each person in turn had to act out the story in his or her own way. When everyone had had a chance, the class as a whole decided who had done the best job of acting. In the process of this final decision, we took the time to discuss what the parable meant. Through involvement in a simple game, people learned important elements of Jesus' teachings.

The December Family Project

Not every course in act two is planned for a limited age group, for children alone or for youth or adults. Some courses attempt to bring together cross-age groups in the same class. The wide age span from the very young to the very old does impose particular restrictions on the activities possible. Yet many people enjoy that span on occasion, at least, and appreciate doing together what can be done.

The December Family Project at South Church may be the best example of cross-age group religious education. (Family project groups were mentioned briefly at the end of chapter 1 in connection with the Christmas pageant celebration.) The parish mailing for Advent in 1972 contained the following description of the project:

> It is for young and old, male and female, singles and couples and families. It is a time to be together in small groups to share the wonder and joy of the Christmas season. . . . This year, during Advent which begins December 3rd, groups can utilize the two-hour Sunday morning time to be together (as well as other times, if they so choose). Groups will meet during the education period and do activities of their choice (a long list of suggested activities will be provided). Then we will gather for celebration and share the experiences of our smaller groups, light an Advent wreath, and sing together.

Families were encouraged to join a group as a unit so that parents and children could share a common experience. For some families in that hectic season these were among the very few times when they ended up doing things together. But others too were invited to become a part of a holiday "extended family"—single persons, widows, grandparents whose children and grandchildren were far away.

Among the popular suggested activities for these groups were the singing of music and the telling of stories. Old familiar Christmas carols (which may not yet be familiar to the youngest children) and newer, unfamiliar carols are good for family groups that like to sing; one person commented that "all participated in the singing (the youngest crying in time with the music)." And Christmas lore is filled with stories which children can enjoy and which adults love the excuse to hear also. One group even found and read together a Christmas folk story told by Martin Luther over four hundred years ago.

These extended families have found new meaning in older rituals and experiences which are often neglected or forgotten today. Worship, for example, is quite different in a small, intimate group from how it is in a large congregation. Someone lights a candle to open the service. A child reads from the Bible, possibly the same Bible she was just given by the church a few months ago on graduation from second grade. Then each person in turn gives a simple prayer. It can be deeply moving for adults to hear the prayers of children, and for a child to hear the prayers of his parents.

The lighting of candles in an Advent wreath (one the first Sunday, two the second, etc.) is a familiar ritual in many congregations. South Church has used that ritual some years as a part of the formal worship service in act one. But the same ceremony can be done in a different and equally meaningful way as a part of celebration. Family groups go through the ritual informally during act two. And in the final act one group may share what it has done with the whole congregation. The ritual then takes on variety from the diversity in the project groups.

Some people are so busy in December that Sunday morning is all they can give to church. But others are able to make time beyond the two-hour program to allow additional opportunities for family groups. A meal in someone's home, Sunday breakfast before church or Sunday supper, a late afternoon tramp in the woods, sitting together around the fire as people toast marshmallows or sip hot cocoa—each of these activities has left happy memories in the minds of the people who participated.

The lists of suggested activities go on: study the symbols of the Christian faith and make decorations for a Christmas tree or for a Jesse tree; bring an unbreakable crèche set and let children rearrange the figures over and over as they learn the Christmas story; share personal memories of significant Christmases past; make a Christmas card to give to the whole church during a

December celebration; share the Advent traditions of other cultures and nations.

Christmastime, too, should be a season in which we look beyond the community of people who are able to come and participate in parish life. One family group did a study of the biblical story of Simeon and Anna (Luke 2:25-38); this elderly man and woman gave special praise to God for the opportunity to see the baby Jesus a few days after his birth. The project group thought about the particular meaning of Christ's coming to those in old age. They then set out to visit a number of elderly people in the parish who were unable to get out to church.

The December family project has already become something of a custom in its few years of existence. That project is a special holiday variation within a broader theme of religious education. The participation of young and old together in a small group learning experience has proved to be a happy way of celebrating Advent.

Planning for the Education Program

The attempt to be both responsible and imaginative in education offerings for all ages requires a lot of planning. And there is an additional need for coordination if the courses of act two are to be integrated with the content of worship and celebration. This critical area of educational administration has undergone considerable development in South Church since the inception of the three-part Sunday morning program.

Central to the planning process from the beginning has been the involvement of lay people in the month-by-month process of creating courses. Membership on the congregation's Board of Education is one of the most demanding organizational responsibilities in the parish. The lay members of the board are charged with the continuing task of reflecting the diverse needs and wishes as regards religious education in the congregation as a whole.

There can be definite value in having a number of people

involved together in creating courses. We have found that imagination is fostered best over the long run when a group of people stimulate each other's thinking rather than when one or two persons work all by themselves.

The nurturing of imagination is also served by the growing dialogue between boards and committees responsible for different parts of the three-act program. The worship perspective of the Board of Deacons is not the same as the perspective of the Board of Education. But as these two boards work together to integrate the total Sunday morning service, their differing points of view keep each of them from settling into unwelcome ruts.

Specifically, the members of the Board of Education try to keep a variety of factors in mind as they plan courses: theological and biblical concerns, the needs and possibilities of various age groups, the potential of available teachers, the issues of the world around us in which people act out their faith, and the mechanical and practical limitations of time and space in the two-hour program and the South Church building.

We have tried assigning individual board members to plan all the courses for one particular age group throughout the year. The board also asked its members another year to take a particular theological theme and develop courses on that theme for various age groups. A third year was organized by asking individuals to take a particular month and coordinate all the courses for every age level in that month; this procedure made it easier to develop a common religious theme for a given month.

The congregation has also been involved in the planning process through all-church workshops, questionnaires, and evaluation sessions. What seems to be most important is that the whole congregation feels that it has an input and a responsibility for act two. Within that basic feeling, no single method of organization seems to be required by the religious education needs of the three-part program.

In addition to lay responsibility for the education program, the involvement of members of the church staff is critical to the process of planning courses. The part-time South Church religious education coordinator is a central participant with the Board of Education in creating new courses. She also has particular responsibility for coordinating the translation of imaginative ideas into actual classes; someone needs to see that teachers are assigned, that the right room is available for a particular class (the candlemaking class, for example, needs to meet in the kitchen where there is a stove), and that necessary materials and resources are gathered ahead of time.

A major share of the responsibility for integrating the courses of act two with worship and celebration also falls on the total church staff. The Board of Deacons works with the minister in developing "any general policies and principles as may be appropriate in relation to the sacraments and the worship life of the church"; but most of the week-to-week planning for the opening worship service is done by the minister and the organist-choirmaster. Full staff meetings are helpful in relating education classes to sermons or choral music and in planning the ways in which each staff person can contribute to the teaching needs of act two.

Putting Act Two Together

At the end of each month a list of the courses to be offered in act two for the following month is mailed out to the parish. Along with course titles is a series of course descriptions, each a paragraph or so in length. Members of the parish are asked to fill out a postcard listing the course preferences of every member of the family and then return the card to the church. Advance notice about the size of each class is needed, in order to plan space, check with teachers, order materials, etc.

Course descriptions include a designated age group. The congregation is reminded that any person may take any course, regardless of the age level listed, but the teachers will be focusing their presentation at the designated level. One grandmother joined the class on the meaning of worship which was planned for grades 4-6; she entered into that course beautifully without overpowering the others, and her comments helped to draw out the children in their learning.

A basic implication in the above mailing and postcard procedure is that Sunday school in South Church involves the element of choice. Each person is able to choose from among a limited number of course offerings. The hope in this cafeteria approach to learning is that freedom of choice will breed quality and interest. Act two might well be described as "free enterprise in religious education."

Giving people a choice has proved to be a problem on occasion when the church offers several attractive courses and a particular individual wants to take more than one class at the same time. We have usually resisted the temptation to scale down the number of interesting offerings in an attempt to spare individuals that difficult decision. Members of the Board of Education have made such comments as "Life is full of choices." We believe it is better usually to offer a variety of attractive options which can appeal to a variety of people than to plan a single course which is intended for everyone.

The Sunday morning bulletin which is given to people as they enter the sanctuary contains the order of worship for act one on the left-hand side. On the right-hand section we list the education courses for that month at the top and a model order for the celebration experience at the bottom. Alongside each course title is room for an age group, a place of meeting, and the person or persons who are teaching that class. Extra copies of the monthly mailing with full course descriptions are available for those who wish to look at them.

Considerable thought has gone into the need to make visitors feel welcome in the three-part program. Unless one stops to think about it, the courses in act two can have the effect of scaring people away. A newcomer at the end of the month may look at the bulletin and see a series of courses which have been meeting for one or more Sundays already; that person may feel that he or she has missed important background material and that without such material there is little point in going to class.

One solution is to plan some courses which build their content from week to week and therefore require regular attendance, but also to plan other courses which start afresh every Sunday. Sermon discussion, a small group experience of prayer, some kinds of Bible study—classes such as these can involve persons who come to church on an irregular basis without making them feel left out because they missed church the week before. If the morning bulletin gives some indication of which classes build on content from the previous week and which classes do not, the visitor may find an easier entry into the education program.

The presence of visitors also requires a special effort on the part of the regular congregation to explain what the three-part program is all about and to let people know what to do and where to go. Should every parish member disperse to a class immediately after worship, the newcomer would be left high and dry, unnoticed and feeling unwelcome.

Assigning a few persons (ushers or others) to stand at the back of the sanctuary after the opening service is a procedure which has helped us to spot the visitor and make him or her feel at home in the total three-part program. It is always possible to introduce the new person to a church member who is already going to a given course and ask the church member to bring the visitor along to class.

Coffee and Juice

One final issue deserves mention, not necessarily because of its inherent importance to religious education but because of its continuing recurrence as a topic of discussion in South Church. If the Deity has a sense of humor (as I hope he does), he must have had abundant opportunity to use it for all of us as we have struggled over refreshments during the three-part program. The congregation has probably spent more time discussing coffee and juice than almost any other aspect of the two hours.

The humor does not come from a hard-working hospitality committee which has struggled for several years to meet the parish's thirst. What brings a smile is the number of functions that refreshments have performed and the number of ways we have tried to fit coffee and juice into the two hours. Someone once suggested a four-part program of worship, education, coffee, and celebration!

At the beginning of the three-part service in 1972, refreshments were served during the intermission between act one and two, but that intermission became so long, with people lingering over coffee, that the education period was cut short. The next proposal was to serve coffee and juice in the sanctuary aisle during the intermission between acts two and three. It was hoped that the refreshments would entice people to come back to celebration.

The parish put up with this use of the sanctuary aisle for about as long as people could stand it. But the chaos of coffee and juice in the aisle—and on the pews—every Sunday became too much. And the effort to call people to worship at the beginning of act three became more and more difficult. Occasional food and drink in church was all right; after all, don't congregations celebrate Communion in the sanctuary? But must we do all that every Sunday?

Inevitably, the refreshments found their way back into the kitchen. Hot water and instant coffee were set out on a table on a do-it-yourself basis. And parish thirst was dignified by becoming a religious education course entitled "Independent, Undecided?" and later, "Coffee, Conversation, and Whatever." People can now come in and fix their coffee anytime they want from the conclusion of act one until noon. (The hospitality committee still tries to serve children to make sure every child gets a drink.) Those who want to stay for fellowship can do so, and those who want to bring their coffee to education or celebration can do that.

Coffee and juice are still a problem and still a topic of conversation. The two-hour program is scheduled too tightly to allow room for an adequate coffee break plus enough time for all three acts. On Communion Sundays the first Sunday of the month, the church does plan for a full-scale coffee hour; there is no education or celebration period that day, only a Communion service at ten o'clock and refreshments and fellowship at eleven. The monthly break of that coffee hour does give everyone an opportunity for unhurried, informal conversation.

It may be that all of us need something tangible as a focus of criticism while we go through a period of change. In that sense coffee and juice may be a blessing in disguise. For a congregation moving into a new program of worship, education, and celebration, it may well have been good that the focus of conversation for those who were independent and undecided was the location of the coffeepot. But if God has had his laughs over our struggles with refreshments, we are beginning to see the humor in these struggles ourselves. And that's a gain. As the wandering Sunday coffeepot has finally resettled in the kitchen, the two-hour program has settled down to stay.

Act Two Leads into Celebration

Planning courses, involving all ages, looking at religious topics and personal relationships—these are important tasks in religious education. But a major share of the faith content in act two is hidden inside what happens spontaneously. God often comes to us in surprises, in the unexpected. If we are to experience God, we need to allow these surprises to happen and to learn how to cultivate them when they do.

There is a great story in Mark 2:1-12 in which Jesus was in the middle of a sermon and a paralytic was lowered through the roof into the room where he was preaching. Jesus used the interruption to teach those present about faith. What often happens with us is that such surprises just sit there ignored as we pass them by. If they are ignored, they may lose their meaning and their power.

Significant things do happen in act two, both planned and

unplanned. Yet if we are to find the faith meaning in those events, we may need to share them in some form with other people—talk about them, reenact them, pray about them, sing about them, laugh or cry about them, wrestle with their mystery together in silence. Sometimes this sharing may happen inside the small group of an education course, and that is good. But the small groups of act two are only one part of the church family. Significant events may also cry out to be shared with the whole church so that we may discover their full meaning as faith possibilities for all of us.

The education period may plant seeds, but the seeds may die without further care. Those same seeds, however, can grow abundantly if we cultivate them. Part of the faith content of act two depends on what happens afterward. The third act of the three-part Sunday morning program can help to fulfill the educational potential of seeds which are planted earlier in the morning. Act two leads us into celebration.

4
Celebration

Several months after South Church had adopted its three-act Sunday morning program, a member of the congregation was asked to comment on the third act, the celebration period. The answer came back, "I'm not sure exactly what celebration is all about, but I think we'd be a little worse off without it."

That response summed up the early feelings of many in the parish. Celebration was the newest part of the two-hour program. And it seemed to be the most difficult part to pin down in a definition or to describe to others outside the congregation. Yet something valuable was beginning to happen in act three, and many could sense that value even if they couldn't put their feelings into words.

In time the church has come up with several statements which help to describe the celebration experience. The weekly Sunday morning bulletin uses the phrase "Open Worship—focusing on Spirit, personal involvement, congregational sharing in faith." Act three can be seen as a cross between an old-fashioned hymn sing and a contemporary happening; on occasion that mixture is flavored by a touch of the medieval morality play.

In more theological terms, celebration is a time when the congregation as a whole seeks to discover and to lift up the sacramental presence of Christ in the totality of human experience. Or, as one woman put it more simply, "That's where the Holy Spirit comes in!"

One member of the Board of Deacons analyzed the final act of the Sunday morning service in the following categories:

> The essential ingredients, in no particular order, include: (*a.*) Fellowship (sense of community and friendship); (*b.*) Sharing (showing concern for the important events in the lives of individuals in the church); (*c.*) Spirit (the feeling that a religious feeling or Holy Spirit is present in the gathering); (*d.*) Dedication (a renewal of spirit for the coming week). Several methods of attaining the ingredients are songs, prayer, verbal communication, physical contact—the semi-spontaneous expressions of individuals under the general guidance of a leader.

Another deacon balanced the analytical tone of that statement with a more psychologically oriented reflection:

> While attention to program is desirable and necessary, I believe that it would be premature and possibly unproductive to become too preoccupied with "how to do it" before we have searched very carefully into our own expectations and hopes, into our resistances and fears, and into our satisfactions and disappointments as they relate to our involvement in celebration. . . . Celebration places demands upon us that are not encountered in the same way or to the same degree in the other parts of the service. A very human reaction to that which is stressful, uncomfortable or unfamiliar, is evasion. Evasion can wear a hundred masks. Until we have worked through our own attitudes and emotions and values to the point that permits us to face the very fundamental questions about our participation in the "celebration" experience, we are not likely to find programs or structures that will meet our own needs or those of others in the congregation.

Others have placed less emphasis on possible inhibitions during act three. Only three months after the inception of the two-hour service one man (who was not at the time on any church board or committee) could write:

At first my feeling on the celebration was a somewhat skeptical "Well, I'd like to see what it's all about." In the weeks we have been trying it, I have experienced an increasing enrichment from the spirit it has generated. I feel now that it opens many important opportunities for sharing individual and group concerns which could not be realized in any other way. I look forward to a further growth and development of the celebration.

Celebration as Congregational Worship

In attempting to sketch out a broad outline for understanding the third act of the three-part service, we need to affirm at the outset that celebration is a form of worshiping God. Part of the difference between the opening service of act one and the final act, however, is that the former is essentially leader-centered worship, while the latter is congregational worship. (Our use of the term *congregational* with a small c distinguishes that word from the religious denomination which calls itself Congregational; both leader-centered and congregational worship, we believe, can be found in Congregational churches, as well as in most other denominations.)

In leader-centered services the basic action is prepared and offered by relatively few leaders. The congregation may join in the singing of hymns or the reading of responses, but the primary responsibility for reenacting the worship drama of salvation is placed in the hands of minister, organist, and choir.

In leader-centered worship members of the congregation enter into that experience primarily as individuals alongside each other. A person coming to church has no fundamental dependence here on the others who are present. Such a service is like a concert or a movie. When people go to a concert, they come in order to hear what is going on up at the front. They may become tremendously absorbed in the music and transformed in mood or outlook by what they hear. But concertgoers are not dependent on relationships with others in the audience in order to get something out of the performance.

It makes very little difference whether the audience at a movie is filled with strangers or friends, except for the few with whom we attend. We do not expect to shake hands with the people in the next row or the next aisle. Nor is there any expectation of a fellowship and coffee hour with the other members of the audience when the show is over. We tune in to what is happening at the front, and we try to tune out most of what is happening around us. It is quite possible to see a movie and remain virtually anonymous to the others in the same room.

The church on occasion consciously chooses leader-centered services which are similar to a concert or a movie. One woman commented to me a few months ago that the reason she goes to worship where she does is because the services in that church are anonymous. This person enjoys being able to slip in and out of the sanctuary unnoticed and to become caught up in whatever part of the worship drama she happens to find meaningful on the particular day. Going to worship at a large cathedral may involve some of the same leader-centered reasons and feelings.

In *congregational* worship, however, the congregation becomes a participant in the basic drama of the service. The persons who are present worship with each other, rather than alongside each other. The quality of such an experience does depend in a fundamental way on who is present (and who is absent) in the congregation, as well as on the depth of personal relationships between the members.

Whereas the stage for the leader-centered worship drama is the chancel up at the front, the stage for a congregational service is the whole sanctuary. The presence of God is symbolized as something between us around which we gather. In congregational worship as we focus on that divine presence we see each other, and vice versa. Other persons are not primarily a potential distraction from our individual relationship with God but rather become a means of deepening that relationship.

Leader-centered worship is like a string of Christmas tree lights wired in parallel, each light on its own private circuit; it is possible for one light to burn out without affecting the other lights on the string because the others have their own circuit. Congregational worship, however, is like Christmas lights wired in series on a single circuit; the brightness of each light is dependent on the amount of electricity which can flow through the whole string.

Congregational worship does not remove the necessity for leadership; but the role of leadership changes from one of acting out the drama for the people to one of leading the people in a corporate reenactment. The drama of worship does not change, though now there are more actors. And a congregational service does not mean the absence of preparation in advance; such would be chaos. Our preparation must leave room for surprises, however, and particularly for the surprise of God's Holy Spirit moving in and through us.

Why would a community of faith want to move beyond a leader-centered service, such as act one at South Church, to a congregational service, such as celebration? The basic reason, I believe, is the simple desire for something more than we have known. Our past is not necessarily wrong, but neither does that past necessarily contain all of the richness possible in a life of faith.

A group of people begin to hunger for something more than emotional or intellectual absorption in a drama which remains essentially "out there." They want to participate in worship, belong to it, feel it as theirs. The congregation reaches out to shape and to be shaped by the continuing experience of the presence of God. And the people want to become involved in that experience as a part of a supportive community, as members of each other as well as members of Christ.

There's an old adage which goes:

> If I hear it, I forget it.
> If I see it, I remember it.
> If I do it, I know it.[1]

Surely that adage can apply to knowing God through worship. If people simply hear a service which is spoken or sung by someone else, they are likely to forget it. If they can see that service acted out in a dramatic way in front of them, these same people will probably remember it. But when persons are caught up themselves in the doing of worship, then is the door opened to the deepest knowledge of God.

Celebration, then, is congregational worship. It may offer a deeper experience of God through human community than the leader-centered service of act one, but this final act also asks more of people. Personal involvement and congregational sharing in faith can be extremely difficult. As in many experiences, a person is able to get out of celebration what he or she is willing and able to put into it.

Yet if celebration is difficult, it comes at the end of a morning of preparation. So often, churches attempt an informal service the first thing on Sunday morning when people have had little or nothing to prepare them. Isn't it better to start with an experience such as formal worship which places fewer demands on a person and then build up to the challenge of congregational worship? The opening service provides balance and perspective, and the education period allows the opportunity for people to become actively involved in small group learning; with both of these acts in the two-hour program fertilizing the ground, celebration has a greater opportunity to take deep root and grow to maturity.

Celebration as Play

Donald E. Miller, Graydon F. Snyder, and Robert W. Neff have written a book about biblical simulations which provides some helpful material to an understanding of the celebration period in the three-part Sunday morning program. Their chapter "Why Use Biblical Simulations?" is equally applicable in parts to the South Church third act:

> Faith is a play of the imagination. It is imagining and hoping in what is not yet seen. It is the fanciful hope of an Abraham whose wife is barren. It is the imaginative vision of a Moses whose people are held

> in Egyptian captivity. It is the dream of a John who records his vision of the end of the age in the book of Revelation. There is a playfulness in the Scriptures that more than anything in Western history has served to release man from the drudgery of his circumstances, from the fatedness of his existence. . . . If the Scripture itself is a record of the playfulness of faith, it would seem that we ought to be more imaginative in our own interpretation of it. Playfulness encourages creativity. Play is not bound by the hard necessities of the work world. Play is more appropriate as an approach to the larger context of life than is work, which is largely means-end activity.[2]

The authors go on to speak of imagination as healing. Imagination is a "gateway to the past," a "healer of the present," and a "door to the future."[3] Speaking about the first of these, they write:

> The past is not merely a set of facts to be verified. One could not know Jesus by documenting all the facts of his life year by year. Nor is the past simply a tradition to be broken, a prison to be escaped, an ignorance to be forgotten. Rather the past is an open possibility to be regained by fantasy and imagination as well as hard research. Celebration and storytelling are how we recover who we are and where we are going.[4]

Obviously, these authors did not have the three-part Sunday morning program at South Church in mind when they wrote. But their ideas are entirely compatible with that program, and particularly with the third act of the service.

An earlier chapter of this book defined the teaching of religion as the ways in which the religious community passes on its own way of life—its history, beliefs, rituals, and traditions—to potential believers or to actual believers who wish to deepen their participation in that way of life. This definition helped to inform the education classes of act two. But if "the past is an open possibility to be regained by fantasy and imagination as well as hard research," the teaching of religion leads us into celebration, too. Indeed, act three may be a fulfillment of the education period if "celebration and storytelling are how we recover who we are and where we are going."

There is ample room in act three to deal with scripture imaginatively. Familiar biblical stories can be acted out with members of the congregation playing different roles through the use of imagination. The point is not necessarily to draw a moral application from scripture. Rather, in playing the story we can feel and understand something of what it has meant to the community of faith in the past to be human in God's world.

Harvey Cox talks about the role of celebration in becoming alive to history:

> Much has been written in recent years about man as a "historical" being, a spirit who perceives himself in time. These analyses have contributed much to our understanding of man. What they often overlook, however, is that our capacity to relate ourselves to time requires more than merely intellectual competence. Well-tabulated chronicles and sober planning alone do not keep us alive to time. We recall the past not only by recording it but by reliving it, by making present again its fears and delectations. We anticipate the future not only by preparing for it but by conjuring up and creating it. Our links to yesterday and tomorrow depend also on the aesthetic, emotional, and symbolic aspects of human life—on saga, play, and celebration. Without festivity and fantasy man would not really be a historical being at all.[5]

To see the final celebration act as play does not mean that this act is unreal or frivolous; play is an important activity for adults and children in which we uncover much of the richness of human life. Celebration is not the same thing as permanent, artificial smiles or manufactured pressure to be bubbly together. Plays can be tragedies as well as comedies. And how often do children play death ("bang, bang, you're dead")? Even in Jesus' day, play involved both joy and sorrow: "But to what shall I compare this generation? It is like children sitting in the market places and calling to their playmates, 'We piped to you, and you did not dance; we wailed, and you did not mourn'" (Matthew 11:16-17).

The celebration period, then, is both a form of congregational worship and a form of play. There need be no contradiction here. A congregational service as we have described it is one in which persons become involved as participants in the basic drama of worship. And one of the ways of involvement is through faith as a play of the imagination. We worship as we enter imaginatively into the roles of penitent or prophet or supplicant.

The ancient psalmists understood this relationship of worship and play. One hears both dimensions in the well-known One Hundred and Fiftieth Psalm:

> Praise the Lord!
> Praise God in his sanctuary;
> praise him in his mighty firmament!
> Praise him for his mighty deeds;
> praise him according to his exceeding greatness!
>
> Praise him with trumpet sound;
> praise him with lute and harp!
> Praise him with timbrel and dance;
> praise him with strings and pipe!
> Praise him with sounding cymbals;
> praise him with loud clashing cymbals!
> Let everything that breathes praise the Lord!
> Praise the Lord!

Celebration as Outreach

A third dimension to an understanding of the celebration period is the element of outreach. Act three is not a time to seek an inclusive, self-contained unity within the church family but is rather an opportunity to open and redirect our worship and our education to the unity we share with the whole family of humanity.

The focus of the celebration is the presence of Christ. It is Christ's Spirit which we are called together to celebrate. But that Spirit is at work in the whole world, not just in the church. In act three we lift up the broken body of the suffering Christ wherever we experience him in human suffering today. And we also rejoice at the new life Christ gives to bring healing out of sickness, hope out of despair, peace out of war, reconciliation out of estrangement. In celebration we affirm the lordship of Christ over the whole of God's creation.

After the congregation has gone through an experience of formal worship and small group learning, we regather to attempt to hold up for all to see what God is doing in Christ today. And the recognition of his presence in the world leads by the very nature of the gospel to the recognition that he calls us to follow him, to continue the ministry begun in Jesus of Nazareth.

If celebration lifts up the Spirit of Christ, then, that lifting up is done in order to make it possible for the church to join him in his work. The community of faith does not bring Christ to the world, for he is already there. But in celebration we give witness to who Christ is and to what he is doing.

There is yet another sense in which celebration and outreach are linked. The Christian is charged to live by faith as "the assurance of things hoped for, the conviction of things not seen" (Hebrews 11:1). Even when the forces of darkness and despair appear to be in control, the church is called to celebrate the victory which is already assured in Christ.

Paul and Silas could celebrate long ago by praying and singing hymns to God after they had been beaten and thrown in prison (Acts 16:11-40). And the civil rights marchers of this country in the early 1960s could celebrate through numerous setbacks by singing "We Shall Overcome." The gift of faith to celebrate at the midnight point of seeming defeat may well be the gift which gives power to the church's outreach.

Celebration, however, is not something that we try to do for God, but something that we let God do in us and through us. As we are caught up in his spirit of joy, that joy overflows and reaches out to those around us. If celebration is related to outreach, it is we who celebrate and God who reaches out through us.

Paul described the life of faith long ago as a life of celebration in the midst of whatever trials and tribulations the world might bring: "Rejoice in the Lord always; again I will say, Rejoice. Let all men know your forbearance. The Lord is at hand. Have no anxiety about anything, but in everything by prayer and supplication with thanksgiving let your requests be made known to God. And the peace of God, which passes all understanding, will keep your hearts and your minds in Christ Jesus" (Philippians 4:4-7).

It should, of course, be obvious that a twenty-minute celebration period at the end of a two-hour Sunday morning program can be no guarantee that a church will be able to "rejoice in the Lord always." The idea of celebration as outreach in the midst of difficulty is a goal toward which to strive, just as the ideas of celebration as congregational worship and as play are goals ahead. Yet act three may well need such high goals if it is to have sufficient direction and motivation to last over the years. It may be that the quality of vision at the beginning of the journey is what is most important to the long-range meaning, value, and success of the actual trip.

The Content of Celebration

The best way to describe the celebration period of the Sunday morning program at South Church is probably through illustrative examples. If the theory is important for long-range vision, concrete illustrations are helpful in trying to get a handle on the specific possibilities in act three. What follows is a description of some of the varieties of content which have already found their way into celebration.

1. *Fellowship.* Personal fellowship is often an indirect result, and the most important result, of an activity aimed at something else. On January 13, 1974, the South Church organist began act three by playing "I Love to Tell the Story" on the piano at the front of the sanctuary. To my knowledge that was the first time anyone had sung that particular hymn in this congregation in several years. It was not that there was anything wrong with it, but rather that the musical style and the theology of the text did not seem to fit the worship tastes of the parish.

Once we had finished that hymn, however, someone in the congregation suggested "Amazing Grace," and then another requested "Give Me That Old-Time Religion." Before people knew it, we were belting out one gospel hymn after another. Most of the congregation couldn't remember the words, and one could hear many la-la-las sung with gusto to familiar tunes while people waited for the words of the chorus to come around again.

Just about everybody had a smile on his or her face. It reminded me of the smile on people's faces when they lick the dasher of an old-fashioned ice-cream maker, the kind you hand crank until the mixture gets too hard to turn; there's no way to lick that dasher without dribbling all over your shirt. Or maybe the smiles were like our reaction to Santa Claus at Christmastime. Which of us adults does not find some thrill of enjoyment at the white beard and the ho-ho-ho and the large, fat stomach—in spite of our maturity and sophistication?

Few members of this Middletown congregation use the language of many of those old gospel hymns when speaking about their faith. No one seemed to take those songs seriously that morning, at least not seriously in the sense of singing them with a look of sober, somber introspection. But it was so much fun to sing those old hymns together, music that many hadn't heard since childhood.

Nobody suggested at the end of that hymn sing that South Church return to a different hymnbook or to a theology that many had worked long and hard to move beyond. Yet I wonder whether the real sign of moving beyond our past is not the ability on occasion to enter into that past and to enjoy it for the moment. When we are afraid to come anywhere near the faith of our childhood, whatever that faith may be, we may still be caught up in that faith, dominated by the need to rebel against it and to let others know we really don't believe all those things. But when we are free of the past, we have little to fear in reliving it once in a while.

What stood out in that celebration period was the sense of

fellowship among those who were present. An old-fashioned hymn sing isn't worth analyzing too much; but it is worth doing. And the twenty minutes of act three that morning gave those who sang and those who smiled a deeper sense of the ties which bind us together in the fellowship of the Holy Spirit.

2. *Healing.* A five-year-old in the parish had spent half of his life wearing a bulky set of leg braces to cure a problem in his hips. The braces meant that he had to move about in a wheelchair or to pull himself around by his hands on the floor. In May of 1973 the braces were removed as the ailment had healed.

On the following Sunday that child came to church and managed to get through the nursery during worship, and the education period. He kept jumping up and down and running around, obviously far more excited about the new use of his legs than about the particular topic of act two. When it was time for celebration, the class came down to the sanctuary; during that final act they got up in front of the congregation to tell people what they were learning.

The five-year-old boy, however, was not interested in what the class was doing. He raised his hand and asked the teacher if he could tell the church something special. She nodded her approval. Then, in a small clear voice, he told the congregation what was on his mind: "I can walk!"

The minister asked him if he could show us. Without a moment's hesitation, the boy started jumping up and down and hopping around the communion table at the front of the sanctuary. The whole church broke out into spontaneous applause. That was a celebration of healing that few present will ever forget.

Other healings may be far less dramatic, but their impact can be just as profound. One man was able to summon the courage to stand up and thank the church for its caring at the time of his son's suicide. On another occasion we heard the good news that a long-time church member had just had a second remission in her bout with leukemia; the congregation celebrated by singing "Now Thank We All Our God."

3. *Religious Festivals.* A year after the unrehearsed Christmas pageant of 1972, the church decided to give a different structure to our celebration of the religious festival of Advent. Family project groups involving people of all ages were formed to meet during act two around eight themes or topics which are basic parts in the Christmas story. And a special celebration of the Christmas story was planned to take place during act three on Sunday, December 23.

No one had a clear idea at the beginning of Advent what that celebration on December 23 would become. What we hoped to do was to fashion a drama out of the developing content of the family education groups. There was no expectation that the drama would pick up every thread in the biblical story; the expectation instead was that our celebration would include something from the experience of every project group.

In the middle of December, representatives from each family group met for an evening to share what their groups were doing and to sketch out a rough outline for the celebration of the Christmas story. Those representatives then took the outline back to their respective groups and let each group know what they were expected to contribute to act three on the twenty-third.

What emerged on Christmas Sunday was a unique event. There was a formal worship service at ten o'clock with special Christmas music, and most people stayed when the service was over. When it was time for act three, the congregation reconvened for a different kind of worship experience.

The family group whose theme was "Angels" led off the celebration period by singing "It Came upon a Midnight Clear"; the congregation was invited to join in the singing. Then three members of that group played "Angels from the Realms of Glory" on their recorders. The group had studied the fact that angels in the Bible were messengers; members of the group now passed out a number of simple messages to the congregation: "Joy to the world," "Peace on earth," "Good will to men and women."

The celebration moved into a "time of awe and wonder" prepared by the group on Old Testament prophecies of the Messiah and the group on the Holy Family. Here the congregation was shown slides depicting the Holy Family according to various famous artists; during the slide show a recording was played of readings from the Old Testament. The mood for this part of the experience was one of reverence.

Another group changed the mood to reflection on the reality of the Incarnation. What was it really like, they wondered, for Mary to travel by donkey while she was pregnant, or for Joseph to be forced to leave his work and flee to Egypt? The questions made people think. They made us remember the hard, cold world into which Jesus was born—the same world which we live in today.

There was an offering of food from the Wise Men group, the kind of food these men might have taken on their journey. Another class with a number of small children sang and acted out "The Little Drummer Boy." And there was an offering of praise from the group which had studied the theme of "light": a dozen slides of spectacular light at sunrise and sunset over the mountains or over a city. The family group on "Simeon and Anna" led the congregation in saying together the concluding benediction of Simeon (Luke 2:29-32).

This 1973 celebration of the Christmas story was less dramatic in many ways than the Christmas pageant of the year before. Yet the process of developing that celebration was probably more meaningful for the congregation than the pageant had been. It was a significant leap of faith to start Advent in 1973 without knowing what the climactic celebration of that season would be and to let the education classes during the month give shape to the celebration as they developed. But the whole congregation took that leap of faith together. The result was that people learned much of the meaning of Christmas by attempting to create a celebration which was appropriate to that religious festival.

4. *Acting Out Biblical Stories.* The most difficult problem

with the Christmas pageant of 1972 was the difficulty in finding a comparable pageant for Lent or Easter. We finally decided that the difficulties were too great. If an unrehearsed pageant was appropriate for Advent, such a format seemed to be fraught with problems at the season in which we remember Jesus' death and resurrection.

The decision that year to give up on a Lenten pageant probably said more about South Church at that point in our history than it did about Lent. By then we had lived with celebration for about a year. People were starting to see its possibilities and to feel its power. But that power could be scary. Could we, or should we, reenact in any way the biblical story of the Crucifixion, or the role of Christ in any of the events of Holy Week? A large number of deacons said no. Some events seemed too potent for celebration reenactment.

Celebration is a time for religious symbols. But these symbols can evoke strong emotion. One needs to be very careful, in dealing with symbols, to understand the emotional content they have for people and to treat that understanding with compassion. It does no good—and some harm—to play with symbols in a callous way. What South Church needed was not an unrehearsed Lenten pageant which magnified the risk that some people would find themselves "in over their heads." What was needed instead was a more structured celebration which reassured the congregation that important boundary lines would be respected.

The celebration of the Easter story for the following year, accordingly, was planned in advance around the biblical story of the Emmaus Road (Luke 24:13-31a). Act three on Easter Sunday was an acting out of that story. No one was asked to play the role of Christ or to act out the Crucifixion. Instead, a narrator read the scripture passage, stopping along the way at various planned points to allow Lenten education classes to interpret what was being said.

In that biblical story, Cleopas and a friend are walking sadly along the road to Emmaus at Easter when Jesus himself draws near and joins them. They do not recognize him, however. He asks why they are so sad, and they tell him of the "things that have happened . . . in these days," the things "concerning Jesus of Nazareth, who was a prophet mighty in deed and word before God and all the people."

Here was an opportunity (at the end of verse 19) for the narrator to stop and let some of the Lenten education classes act out some of the mighty deeds or tell of some of the mighty words in Jesus' life. Since the church's Board of Education had known at the beginning of Lent the basic structure of the Easter celebration, it had planned its courses so that some would be prepared to fit into act three when we came to this point and to other points in Luke's account.

The Emmaus Road story concludes: "When he was at table with them, he took the bread and blessed, and broke it, and gave it to them. And their eyes were opened and they recognized him." Several persons had baked bread ahead of time, and they brought their loaves into church to share with the congregation. At the end of act three we stood to sing "Christ the Lord Is Risen Today" and to share with each other a traditional Easter greeting: "Christ is risen"—"He is risen, indeed!"

Other biblical stories are less complex to act out in celebration. The one Lenten story which the congregation has been able to celebrate with no difficulty at all has been the account of Palm Sunday; it is a moving experience for young and old to process around the sanctuary waving palms and carrying banners. And the Old Testament is filled with a variety of stories, such as the one about Noah and the ark, which come alive as they are reenacted.

5. *Important Church Events.* A women's society in the parish donated the money, and several persons donated their time and skill, to build new library shelves in the social room. On May 13, 1973, we decided to move the books from their old location and to dedicate the new library.

At the beginning of celebration that morning everyone was asked to walk up to the old library and pick up one or more books. Even the very youngest and the very oldest members of the parish were to carry something, if only a small volume. And others could bring an armful or a carton. The whole library was moved in less than ten minutes, with all present feeling that they had had a part in what was happening. Act three concluded with a brief dedication service of prayer and song and the gift of a memorial plaque.

Earlier that year the parish dealt with another important church event, the operating budget for 1973 and its implications. The celebration period on January 21 was the congregational meeting called to decide on the budget. This merging of celebration and congregational meeting was not simply a matter of convenient scheduling; it was also an effort to infuse the discussions of church business with the spirit of congregational worship.

Many felt afterward that the attempt was not wholly successful. The mood of the meeting was responsive to inflation and fuel bills, but it seemed to be less open to a celebration of the presence of Christ in the midst of these difficult problems. Yet there seemed to be value in trying to use act three in this way. The same attempt was made for the church's budget meetings in 1974 and 1975.

6. *Coordination with Education Courses.* The Christmas celebration for 1974 (the successor to the Christmas pageant of 1972 and the celebration of the Christmas story of 1973) was planned as a presentation of *Amahl and the Night Visitors* by Gian Carlo Menotti. The solo work in music and dance for that dramatic presentation was rehearsed at a time other than Sunday morning. But much of the preparation for the special celebration was done in coordination with the religious education program in the parish.

Amahl, for example, requires a shepherds' chorus. That chorus was planned as an education class on Sunday mornings beginning in October. People of all ages who wanted to sing in the chorus could do so simply by coming to a course in act two during which the music was learned. And congregational support for sets or costumes—and possibly for refreshments in the intermission before the celebration period that final Sunday—could also be enlisted through the education period (with some help from people outside of the two-hour program).

7. *Development of Celebration Rituals.* The passing of the Peace of Christ between members of the congregation has become an important part of the celebration experience. The minister begins by saying, "The Peace of Christ be with you," and the congregation responds, "And with you also." Then all are free to greet each other with that same formal greeting or an informal variation, and with a handshake or an embrace. The ritual is an important way to include people and to make an individual feel welcome within a spirit of worship. And the passing of the Peace to young children can be especially moving, for them and for the person who shares it with them.

After a retreat in February of 1973 which focused on deepening human relations within the parish, we tried a variation of the Peace. People would greet each other with "I appreciate you because. . . ," followed by whatever made us appreciate that particular individual.

Musical rituals have been important, too. The round "Shalom Chaverim" has often served as a closing benediction at the end of the celebration, sometimes with people holding hands in a circle around the communion table. And special theme songs at the beginning of act three can call people together and relate our celebration to the themes of worship or education.

8. *Allowing Room for Spontaneity.* As the congregation returned for celebration one Sunday, people noticed that a boy in grade school was picking out simple tunes on the piano. He was just learning to play. Someone asked him if he would accompany us as we sang a few hymns. The answer was an obviously pleased affirmative. He could play only the melody line, but the opportunity to do even that for the whole church was a personal high point.

In April of 1973 the Board of Deacons decided to change the arrangement of the front pews in the sanctuary in order to encourage spontaneous sharing between people. Prior to that time these pews sat in parallel rows facing towards the front. All one could see from any pew was the backs of the heads of the people who were closer to the front. But the deacons agreed to turn the three front pews at a forty-five-degree angle, facing inward, and to bring the communion table down from the raised platform in the chancel to the floor at the front of the sanctuary.

The meaning of the change was spelled out in the Sunday morning bulletin:

> The arrangement of the front pews and the communion table is intended to symbolize in a physical way the spiritual meaning of Christian fellowship, with Christ's presence among us down at the level of our common humanity and with the church community gathered around that presence. We hope this physical setting may open the spiritual opportunity of our becoming more fully "united with Christ and one another" in our worship.

The front pews now form a V-shape, with more room for celebration happenings. People can see and hear each other more easily. And the communion table in the middle of the V-shape serves as a focal point for much of the experience of act three. A major effect of this seating change has been an encouragement of spontaneous sharing in celebration.

9. *Reacting to Important Events in the World.* A significant number of people throughout this country were deeply disturbed by the firing of Archibald Cox as Watergate special prosecutor. That firing took place on a Saturday night—October 20, 1973. There was little opportunity to deal with that event in South Church during the first two acts of the Sunday morning program. But by celebration time people needed to share their feelings and reactions.

A number of people spoke of their disturbance. One person suggested that we express our feelings through the words of an ancient psalm read responsively, first by one half of the congregation and then by the other half. Psalm 37 was mentioned:

Fret not yourself because of the wicked,
  be not envious of wrongdoers!
For they will soon fade like the grass,
  and wither like the green herb. . . .

Be still before the Lord, and wait patiently for him;
  fret not yourself over him who prospers in his way,
  over the man who carries out evil devices! . . .

The wicked plots against the righteous,
  and gnashes his teeth at him;
but the Lord laughs at the wicked,
  for he sees that his day is coming. . . .

Depart from evil, and do good;
  so shall you abide for ever.
For the Lord loves justice;
  he will not forsake his saints. (Vv. 1, 2, 7, 12, 13, 27, 28)

The passionate reading of that psalm gave many a feeling of release and a sense of perspective. Celebration didn't solve the problems of corruption in high places, but it did remind us at the very least that others in the past have found strength in their faith to live responsibly through corrupt times.

The celebration period, and the whole three-part program, also took on a potent outreach dimension on another Sunday in 1973. The Board of Education had planned a February course on American Indians to be taught by a high school student who had a particular interest and knowledge in that topic. During the month the class learned a simple Indian tune and an Indian dance.

On the last Sunday of the month the opening worship service included two special anthems, an Indian lullaby, and a Dakota melody called "Indian Hymn of Praise." The altar cloth for that day was a beautiful Navajo rug. During act three, the class which had studied American Indians taught the whole congregation the tune and dance they had just learned. Anyone who wanted to do so was invited to sing and to dance around the communion table. At the end of the morning we were to receive a special offering for native Americans.

That celebration period would have been a moving experience on any Sunday. Those who participated developed a deeper sensitivity to the customs and the rituals of an oppressed people. But that Sunday had special potency because it took place against the backdrop of the sit-in by American Indians at Wounded Knee, South Dakota. The sit-in was going on that very day.

Members of the congregation stated that they did not want to identify with all the tactics and methods of that particular protest. But many did express sympathy for the kinds of grievances which lay behind such protests. The simple tune and dance of that celebration provided an opportunity for symbolic identification with significant grievances.

10. *Celebrating in Different Places.* Act three is normally planned for the sanctuary in order to give celebration the worship atmosphere of that room. But the Spirit of Christ is hardly limited to the church building. The Spirit may be found in places of business or government, in the ghetto and on the farm, in people's homes and on the streets. Christ's presence may be celebrated wherever he is.

We have much room for growth in finding a variety of places in which to hold our celebration. But some progress has been made. One thinks of the time a well-loved member of South Church died after a long illness. She had served the parish in many ways over the years, including a substantial period of time as church librarian. Along with her husband she also loved the out-of-doors. The grounds around their house are a joy to see.

This woman died on Saturday, May 18, 1974. The next day the congregation decided to hold a brief memorial service for her during celebration. The sky was clear blue outside, and the sun was warm and bright; so people walked across the street to the South Green for celebration. The service was simple—a brief prayer, a time of silence, the singing of a hymn that she loved, and the opportunity to share with each other something of the same Peace of Christ which had claimed her beyond death. The mood was one of rejoicing in the midst of tears.

11. *Seasons of the Year.* On the last Sunday of October in 1973 one of the members of the church brought with him a number of cornstalks, pumpkins, and gourds from the family farm. Celebration that day was a time for a number of people to build a harvest display out of this produce up at the front of the sanctuary.

The cornstalks were tied together in the shape of a cone, something like the poles of an Indian tepee. Then the pumpkins and gourds were stacked and arranged in and around the cone. The whole display was left up for a couple of weeks, a visual reminder of the autumn harvest.

12. *Important Personal Events.* A distinguished member of the church, a retired minister, reached his ninetieth birthday on January 29, 1974. On the Sunday beforehand the congregation held a special celebration service in his honor. A children's class had made a paper crown, which they brought forward to place on his head. The congregation was invited to give spontaneous testimony to what this man had done in his life, and a number of people responded. One of the deacons had baked a birthday cake for all to share. And the guest of honor was invited to give the concluding benediction.

Baptism, too, is an important personal event. Sometimes a family prefers the service of baptism during the formal worship of act one, but on occasion such a service seems more appropriate in the informal atmosphere of celebration. One family had their baby baptized during the opening service but planned to celebrate the event in a special way at the end of the morning. The day before the baptism the baby's family, including his older brothers and sisters, baked several batches of cookies. During celebration the next day they passed these cookies out to the whole congregation as a way of sharing their joy with others.

On many occasions the sharing of personal events is simple

and brief. A father once held up his one-year-old daughter to celebrate the fact that she had taken her first steps. We rejoiced when a member of the congregation who had been unemployed was able to find a job. Visiting family or friends have been introduced and welcomed. And people have used act three to affirm graduations, weddings, anniversaries.

The Model Order for Celebration

The content which is possible during the celebration period is rich and varied. But how does the congregation move into this content? How does act three get started? How does the church discover its abilities to celebrate and find the material worth celebrating?

Our answer to these questions is found in part in the model order for celebration which is printed in the weekly bulletin. Act three, to be sure, is an informal service. But we have found it useful to present a general, overall structure for that period within which we believe that celebration is most likely to occur. The model order is not a rigid requirement but is rather an order from which to deviate as our worship is led by the Holy Spirit.

The South Church use of the phrase *model order* seems to be akin to Harvey Cox's description of a "liberating ritual":

> A liberating ritual is one that provides the formal structure within which freedom and fantasy can twist and tumble. It provides the person with a series of movements in which he is given access to an enormous wealth of human feelings. But these feelings now become the material for his own escapades in creativity. The best analogy to a liberating ritual may still be the jazz combo or dixieland band. The chord structure and rhythm conventions provide the base from which spectacular innovations and individual *ad libs* can spin out. Without such a structure, the music would deteriorate into cacophony. With it, the individual players not only climb to musical peaks, but often they stimulate each other to explore unexpected vistas of sound.[6]

This congregation's regular printed order for the third act of the three-part program might well be described in similar terms as "the formal structure within which" the "freedom and fantasy" of celebration "can twist and tumble."

The model celebration order is as follows:

Music.

The Invitation to celebrate.

The Peace of Christ is shared.

The Consecration of Christ's presence in our lives.

The Commission to serve God throughout the week.

Benediction and Musical Response.

The components of this structure are borrowed from the service of the Sacrament in Holy Communion. The context, however, is broadened from a celebration of the presence of Christ in the bread and the wine to a celebration of his presence in the whole of human life.

A typical third act opens with music. The organist plays a familiar hymn or carol on the piano at the front of the sanctuary. As people hear the music in various education classes throughout the building, they prepare to bring those classes to a conclusion for the day; sometimes a child is asked to walk through the halls of the church with a small bell to ring, letting people know that the celebration period is beginning.

As people regather out of the small groups of act two, they may join in singing a verse or two of the hymn being played. Then the celebration leader (who may be the minister or someone else) gives an invitation to join in the celebration. The invitation is a form of call to worship, though the style is more informal than the opening preparation of the ten o'clock service.

Celebration can happen only if the community comes together freely. The Holy Spirit cannot be summoned on command; as Jesus put it, "The wind blows where it wills, and you hear the sound of it, but you do not know whence it comes or whither it goes; so it is with every one who is born of the Spirit" (John 3:8). The invitation to celebrate must respect this basic freedom. The congregation should be encouraged to participate in act three but be reassured that people are free to enter in, or not, in whatever way they wish. All are welcome to join, but no one's arm will be twisted.

The sharing of the Peace of Christ which follows is a time-honored way of letting persons open themselves to each other and to Christ's presence. The church may recall here Jesus' words to his disciples: "Peace I leave with you; my peace I give to you; not as the world gives do I give to you. Let not your hearts be troubled, neither let them be afraid" (John 14:27). The Letter to the Colossians is also helpful background: "And let the peace of Christ rule in your hearts, to which indeed you were called in the one body. And be thankful" (Colossians 3:15).

The central action of the celebration period is usually the consecration. The leader may introduce this section with an open-ended question: "Are there significant events or relationships or objects from your lives which you wish to consecrate? Are there important things that have happened to you or around you that you wish to share?"

Sometimes that question is met with silence, and nothing happens. In that case we move on to the next part of the celebration. But the vast majority of times someone will have something to share. The sharing may have been planned in advance, or it may be more spontaneous.

When something has been shared, the congregation may look for an appropriate way to consecrate that sharing, to lift up the faith meaning in what has been said or done. Here we may pray or sing, laugh or cry, dance or clap our hands, or simply ponder the mystery of faith in silence. Consecration cannot be forced or contrived. It may take time. We cannot expect a mountaintop experience every Sunday. What the church is saying during this period is that Christ is present not just back there in the Bible but also right here in our lives today, if we can only learn how to look for him, sense him, listen for him. Through consecration, in short, our life becomes a part of God's story.

As the time of consecration runs its course, the leader asks if anyone present would like to give the commission. We have worshiped, learned, and celebrated together; now what are we going to do about our faith throughout the week ahead? It was St. Paul who reminded us long ago, "So we are ambassadors for Christ, God making his appeal through us" (2 Corinthians 5: 20a).

A familiar dismissal at the end of the service of Holy Communion is "Go in peace, to love and serve the Lord." The commission at the end of act three is similar to that dismissal. The attempt is usually made, however, to be less general. If at all possible, someone tries to phrase a commission for the coming week which grows out of the specific content of the Sunday morning program on that particular day.

The closing benediction reaffirms God's continuing presence with us wherever we go. That benediction brings act three to a close; but it also serves to bring the entire three-part program to a conclusion. The congregation may join in a musical response to the benediction—a doxology, a verse from one of the hymns used in the opening service, a familiar piece such as "Shalom Chaverim."

A Balance of Planning and Spontaneity

Celebration requires a balance between planning in advance and spontaneity. Too little planning can lead to an experience of chaos or emptiness of little value. Yet too much planning can destroy the spirit of spontaneous worship which the church is trying to cultivate in act three.

The planning procedure which we have developed at South Church consists in encouraging individuals or groups with ideas of things to do in celebration to tell those ideas ahead of time to the minister. These advance suggestions then serve as a pool of possibilities out of which the celebration experience itself can be drawn.

No guarantees are given ahead of time that any particular

suggestion will be implemented. The general response of the minister is something like "I will keep your idea in mind; we will use it if the mood and the context are appropriate when we get into the actual celebration on Sunday morning."

Suggestions involving small children are usually given priority in advance planning, if at all possible. If the teacher for the three-, four-, and five-year-olds comes up with an idea for her class to do something in act three, that suggestion is placed at the head of the list. Small children are usually least able to handle disappointment if something they have been counting on does not actually take place in celebration. Even if the sharing is a simple "show-tell" time, for children to show what they have made and to tell the whole congregation about it, the experience is important to those children and for their growing sense of belonging within the church family.

On occasion, too many ideas are proposed in advance, so that there will obviously not be enough time to follow through on every one in a brief twenty minutes on Sunday. It is also possible that no ideas, or only one or two, will be suggested during the week. There have been celebration periods with little life or spark when we have lived with uncreative silences and even brought things to a close a few minutes early; but the church hasn't worried about those times over the long run.

Often, a concern may come up on the spur of the moment which the congregation may decide to pursue in act three. When the Spirit moves the church in that way, it is quite possible that few, if any, of the ideas thought about in advance will be used on that day. Advance planning, then, is the process of fertilizing the ground out of which possible celebration events can grow.

The procedure of asking people to share their ideas for celebration with the minister before Sunday morning is useful in another way. When many ideas first come in, not enough thought has been given to the crucial question *how* the congregation can participate in celebrating that particular concern. If there is still time before Sunday, however, the minister or another staff person can work on refining the idea with the individual who presented it.

Celebration is not simply having one person stand up and talk about something on his or her mind while everyone else sits passively listening. This third act involves a constant search to find an appropriate way to include people in the experience of celebrating. Advance planning may be particularly helpful in thinking through what is an appropriate way to include this congregation in this particular concern.

In working out the question of how to celebrate a particular experience, we have found that it is better to avoid gimmicks. Some ways of celebrating give the illusion of quick success but may substitute the manipulation of people's emotions and experience for the much deeper and more difficult involvement of the whole person in the worship of God.

Jesus' parable of the sower (Mark 4:1-9) is relevant to the experience of celebration. It is possible to develop exciting events in act three which are similar to the seed which fell on rocky ground, "where it had not much soil, and immediately it sprang up, since it had no depth of soil; and when the sun rose it was scorched, and since it had no root it withered away." Other experiences of celebration may grow more slowly, but because they grow in good soil their final yield may be "thirtyfold and sixtyfold and a hundredfold."

A final word on advance planning: It is possible to be stimulated creatively by the ideas of other churches and other groups, but each congregation will probably need to develop its own particular style of celebration before too long. Every parish has its own personality. Some ideas which have worked beautifully in other congregations would not work at all in South Church; and I'm sure that ideas which have made sense in this Middletown parish would not transplant very well to another church.

Celebration is shaped by the culture and the life-styles of the people who are called to celebrate. For such an experience to grow, it must be based on integrity. In more theological terms, act three has been built on the idea of freeing the life of the Holy Spirit from within rather than on attempting to imitate the life of the Spirit as it is perceived in others. Celebration involves freeing the gift, and the gifts, of the Spirit which are given at baptism but which, in most of us, are almost unused and even unrecognized.

Advance ideas for celebration, then, come in from a variety of sources—from individual church members, from education classes, from the world outside the church, from other churches. These ideas are refined and organized. They provide the background against which the third act of the three-part program actually occurs.

Celebration as the Participation of Amateurs

There is a growing interest in the life of celebration within the wider church. A number of books have been written recently on the topic. And committees have been formed to look into ways of stimulating religious celebrations. That interest is to be welcomed and encouraged.

Much of that interest, however, seems to focus on celebration as the performance of professionals. A number of celebrations have been designed and written up which require people with special talent and training to put them on. And many of these could take weeks or months to develop and rehearse.

Such dramatic experiences are a legitimate part of the meaning of celebration. Some of the content of the third act in the South Church Sunday morning program fits this description. For example, the performance of Menotti's *Amahl and the Night Visitors* as the Christmas celebration of 1974 called for several solo parts to be done by individuals with both talent and time for rehearsal.

But the celebration period could not survive week in and week out if its basic intent were limited to the idea of professional performances. The time factor alone would rule out such an idea. Given everything else that does and should happen in the life of a church and its people, there would not be enough hours between Sundays to prepare a polished performance for act three every week. The more elaborate the preparation needed, the less often the actual celebrations would take place.

It is important, too, to keep the organizational machinery which supports the celebration period at a manageable level. The advance planning procedures which South Church has developed for the third act are relatively simple at present; staff and committee responsibilities have not proved to be too great. Yet elaborate celebrations and extensive rehearsals on a regular basis would soon turn the final act of Sunday morning into a bureaucratic nightmare.

The issue is more fundamental than limited time or minimum organization, however. Celebration must be more than a performance by a few talented individuals, because the church is filled with many whose talents are ordinary or limited. Act three must include the participation of amateurs who are moved by the Holy Spirit to celebrate in simple, human, unsophisticated ways.

The South Church program is not an attempt to develop a celebration to end all celebrations. Our goal instead is to set aside a regular period of time in which the church may gradually learn to celebrate the presence of Christ in the whole of human life. Week by week, the congregation grows through experience toward that goal.

Twenty minutes seems so short, but it is amazing how important those few minutes have come to be in the total life of the parish. Celebration is not only what actually happens in act three; it is also what happens to the faith of people who know that there is an act three at a climactic point in the congregation's Sunday morning experience every week.

Those twenty minutes are truly open-ended. Perhaps that's one of the reasons why I've grown to feel a special warm spot in my life for celebration. Worship and education are important, too, of course; each is essential, I believe, to the quality of the overall experience of the church. But celebration is so delightfully unpredictable. Even when act three falls flat on its face, one can feel like celebrating the failure.

Then there's the moment when a small child turns to the congregation and says, "I can walk." With his leg braces off, he bounces and hops and jumps all around the front of the sanctuary. That's celebration.

5
Communion Background

Several years ago, the congregation here in Middletown seemed to accept without question a particular attitude toward the Lord's Table. It was almost assumed that prior approval from the church's Board of Deacons was necessary for any activity involving that table other than the Lord's Supper. Once a month it was spread with a white tablecloth and set with silver communion trays. For the rest of the time it usually sat in solitary splendor up in the chancel with nothing but an altar cloth resting on its solid wooden surface.

The two-hour program has gradually changed this feeling—as has the decision to move the communion table down from the chancel to the floor at the front of the sanctuary. The table has become the central focus of celebration every Sunday. It is still set with a white cloth and silver trays on the first Sunday of the month, but it holds a variety of other things on the other Sundays when the church is engaged in our service of worship, education, and celebration.

On September 15, 1974, for example, the Sunday after President Gerald Ford had given a full pardon to Richard Nixon, the minister read a letter that he had written to President Ford. The letter attempted both to express disagreement with the timing of the pardon and to reaffirm prayer and support in the midst of disagreement for the new president who had taken office at such a difficult time. The letter was written in the first person singular, but space was left at the bottom for other individuals who wished to join in the substance of the letter to add their names. At the end of the sermon the letter was placed on the communion table and left there during education and celebration for others to read and respond to in any way they wished.

Another Sunday, a group was sewing a banner in the social room during the education period, a banner including the words of that famous prayer by St. Francis of Assisi which begins, "Lord, make me an instrument of your peace." A separate class in the sanctuary that day was learning new hymns for celebration. The first group decided on the spur of the moment that it would be more enjoyable to sew while they were listening to music, and they moved their materials in onto the communion table. For the rest of acts two and three, anyone who wanted to participate in that banner and its message could gather around the table and pick up a needle and thread.

When the braided rug class completed its work, the rug was consecrated by laying it on the Lord's Table as a special altar cloth for that celebration period. Again, the table served in the fall of 1974 as the gathering point in the middle of an imaginary Noah's Ark for young and old acting out various animals in a celebration of that biblical story. And the sturdy frame of the same table has supported many offerings, such as the layettes collected during Advent of 1973 to be distributed by a social worker in the congregation to underprivileged children.

The church still has a strong feeling of reverence for the communion table. But our understanding of what reverence means has changed in the past few years. The table has become important more and more as the fundamental gathering point for the community of faith. Reverence for that special wooden piece of furniture is now related to the quality and the variety of the experiences which take place on or around it.

The communion table has come to symbolize the relationship between the three-part Sunday morning program and the service of Holy Communion. The three-part service has not de-emphasized or downgraded the importance of the Lord's Supper. The opposite is true, in fact. Because Christ's presence has been celebrated in so many ways around the Lord's Table in the three-act program, it becomes even more significant to celebrate that presence there in the climactic experience of the Eucharist.

Holy Communion, in short, can be seen as the first among many celebrations of Christ's Spirit. There is a definite relationship between Communion and celebration, between Communion and the full service of worship, education, and celebration. In filling out the larger vision behind the three-part program, we can benefit from a brief examination of the Communion background to that program. That background is found in some of the ideas about the Lord's Supper in the First Letter of Paul to the Corinthians.

Discerning Christ's Presence

> But in the following instructions I do not commend you, because when you come together it is not for the better but for the worse. For, in the first place, when you assemble as a church, I hear that there are divisions among you; and I partly believe it, for there must be factions among you in order that those who are genuine among you may be recognized. When you meet together, it is not the Lord's supper that you eat. For in eating, each one goes ahead with his own meal, and one is hungry and another is drunk. What! Do you not have houses to eat and drink in? Or do you despise the church of God and humiliate those who have nothing? What shall I say to you? Shall I commend you in this? No, I will not.
>
> For I received from the Lord what I also delivered to you, that the Lord Jesus on the night when he was betrayed took bread, and when he had given thanks, he broke it, and said, "This is my body which is for you. Do this in remembrance of me." In the same way also the cup, after supper, saying, "This cup is the new covenant in my blood. Do this, as often as you drink it, in remembrance of me." For as often as you eat this bread and drink the cup, you proclaim the Lord's death until he comes.

> Whoever, therefore, eats the bread or drinks the cup of the Lord in an unworthy manner will be guilty of profaning the body and blood of the Lord. Let a man examine himself, and so eat of the bread and drink of the cup. For any one who eats and drinks without discerning the body eats and drinks judgment upon himself. That is why many of you are weak and ill, and some have died. But if we judged ourselves truly, we should not be judged. But when we are judged by the Lord, we are chastened so that we may not be condemned along with the world.
>
> So then, my brethren, when you come together to eat, wait for one another—if any one is hungry, let him eat at home—lest you come together to be condemned. About the other things I will give directions when I come. (1 Corinthians 11:17-34)

The words of institution for the service of Holy Communion (1 Corinthians 11:23-26) are found in the middle of this discussion by St. Paul of a problem in the first-century church of Corinth. Like many congregations today that parish was in the habit of meeting for church suppers. But the mood at those suppers in Corinth was far from the fellowship of the Holy Spirit.

One family would bring their meal and sit down immediately in a corner of the place of meeting to eat it. A second group might arrive a few minutes later and begin eating in another corner. By the time the whole congregation had gathered together, some of its members were already drunk. And others whose poverty kept them from being able to bring enough to eat were still hungry.

If anyone were to walk into that Corinthian supper from the outside, he or she would have seen very little in people's behavior to remind him or inform her of Jesus Christ and of the life he called his followers to lead. The selfish individualism of the members of that church was a living contradiction of Jesus' statement to the disciples, "This is my commandment, that you love one another as I have loved you" (John 15:12). The least that people could have done was to share their food with each other, so that everyone would be fed adequately.

Paul was upset. He reminded the parish of the tradition he had received from the Lord about Jesus' Last Supper on the night before his death. Then, with that tradition in mind, Paul went on to say, "Whoever, therefore, eats the bread or drinks the cup of the Lord in an unworthy manner will be guilty of profaning the body and blood of the Lord." It is logical to assume that the "unworthy manner" which Paul referred to is the selfish individualism of the parish, which he had talked about just a few verses earlier.

The letter goes on, "For any one who eats and drinks without discerning the body eats and drinks judgment upon himself." That verse is difficult to interpret. In its context, however, I believe that it is reasonable to understand Paul as referring to the importance of discerning the presence of Christ in the body of believers as they eat and drink in his name.

Elsewhere in the same letter Paul described the church as the body of Christ: "Now you are the body of Christ and individually members of it" (1 Corinthians 12:27). When the Corinthian parish gathered in Christ's name for one of its fellowship suppers, the congregation was a part of the living body of Christ. The Spirit of Christ was present in their midst. The mistake of those Corinthian Christians was that they didn't recognize who they were. They didn't see themselves as a part of Christ's body, nor did they discern his presence in their gathering.

Had the church discerned the presence of Christ in the gathered body of believers, its people would not have acted in the selfish and insensitive way they did, with some having too little food and others too much wine. The recognition of Christ's presence in the community of faith brings with it the demand that that community act in a way which allows the presence to shine through its life together.

Probably few persons in contemporary society would go along with Paul's particular diagnosis as to why some Christians were weak and ill and why some had died. But the general point of the whole passage is still valid: If you are members of the church, then act like it.

To tie the whole discussion together, Paul concludes, "So

then, my brethren, when you come together to eat, wait for one another—if any one is hungry, let him eat at home—lest you come together to be condemned." If someone is so hungry that he or she cannot physically wait for everyone to gather in church before starting to eat, that person ought to grab a bite to eat at home before coming. Then the congregation will be more able to behave in its gatherings in a way that would bring honor and glory to Jesus Christ.

Communion as Standard

The way in which these arguments of First Corinthians are stated is significant. The words of institution appear right in the center as an integral part of the discussion. The Maundy Thursday Communion meal of Jesus and the disciples becomes the historical reason in back of Paul's anger at the church. It also provides the rationale for describing what is so bad about the actions of the Corinthian congregation. If Christ, himself, promised to be present in the sharing of bread and wine, then the church dare not disregard him in its fellowship suppers.

Nowhere does Paul state or imply that the *only* valid activity of the church would be for its people to gather for the sole purpose of eating the bread and drinking the wine of the Lord's Supper. Nor is there any implication that Christ's presence is limited to that one activity alone. The Spirit of Christ is a living presence in all that the church does. Paul can write elsewhere, "So, whether you eat or drink, or whatever you do, do all to the glory of God" (1 Corinthians 10:31).

Paul's discussion does imply, though, that the particular events of Jesus' Last Supper with the disciples before his death provide an important standard against which to measure the presence of Christ in other areas of life. Indeed, the pivotal significance of the Communion meal for the whole Christian church and the fundamental symbolism it includes suggest that Communion may be the critical and irreplaceable yardstick which Jesus' followers can use in finding and celebrating Christ's presence in the world.

The living Christ is present, according to Paul, as the church recalls his words at the Last Supper and repeats his actions by sharing the bread and the cup in his name. Having this insight into Christ's presence in Communion, the church can begin to discover the larger presence of the Christ in the whole of life. Communion is a kind of litmus test which enables the church to recognize the Risen Lord at work in the world and to give witness to him.

Communion and the Three-Part Program

St. Paul's discussion of the Communion meal in First Corinthians is important background for the South Church program of worship, education, and celebration that we have been describing and illustrating in this book. That program takes the church into diverse and wide-ranging activities. But it is Holy Communion which serves as the basic standard to enable the church to seek out and to celebrate Christ's presence in all that it does.

The warnings given to the church of Corinth need to be taken seriously. A parish ought not to eat and drink in the unworthy manner of selfish individualism. Yet surely Communion can be more than a negative standard for ruling out those activities which are inconsistent with a Christian life. What about the activities which the church may do in a *worthy* manner?

The mistake of the Corinthian Christians, as we have seen, was that they did not see themselves as a part of Christ's body or recognize his presence in their midst. But suppose they had recognized that presence? What might they have done then? The statement "If you are members of the church, then act like it" can be read in a positive as well as a negative way. What can a congregation do which will not only keep it from bringing dishonor to Christ but also enable it to bring honor and glory to his name?

The three-part Sunday morning program is one attempt to answer questions such as these. Wide-ranging and varied church activities whose content reflects the diversity of life itself are one way of bringing to the Lord of life the honor and glory which are his due.

None of the three acts operates with an uncritical acceptance of the idea that anything goes, however. Diverse content by itself could as easily bring dishonor as honor, shame as glory. Some standard is necessary to sift out the good from the bad. And Communion provides that standard. The way in which Christ is present in the Lord's Supper helps the church to understand the broader way in which he is present in worship, education, and celebration.

The Idea of Sacrament

The discussion of the presence of Christ in Communion and in the three-part Sunday morning program brings us now to the idea of a sacrament. Evelyn Underhill defines that idea as follows: "A sacrament is a significant deed, a particular use of temporal things, which gives to them the value of eternal things and thus incorporates and conveys spiritual reality. Hence sacraments involve an incarnational philosophy; a belief that the Supernatural draws near to man in and through the natural."[1] The biblical promise that Christ draws near to us through the natural world of a meal of bread and wine is the reason why Communion is sometimes called the Sacrament.

But the Eucharist does not exhaust the possibilities in the world of sacraments: "Indeed, many of the common things and acts of daily existence can be given such sacramental quality, by the Godward intention of those who are accustomed to seek and find the Eternal in the temporal; and so woven into the fabric of the worshipping life."[2]

When the leader of the celebration act of the three-part service asks the congregation to share significant events or objects or relationships as vehicles of a deepening of faith, he or she is asking people "to seek and find the Eternal in the temporal." The third act in particular is created around the belief that life in its entirety is a sacrament.

Underhill points out that there are dangers in sacraments; the risks, however, are worth taking:

> Therefore the cultus which excludes sacraments does not in consequence draw nearer to God; but renounces a sovereign means by which He is self-imparted to us, and in and through which His action may be recognized and adored. It is true that sacramental methods are always open to the dangers of formalism and exteriorization, and may even slide down into a crass materialism. Yet on the other hand, it is those who have reached out through the sensible to an apprehension of the supra-sensible, who realize most fully the deep mystery and unexhausted possibilities which abide in the world of sense, and therefore its power of conveying to us that which lies beyond, and gives to it significance and worth.[3]

Speaking in particular about the Christian faith, she concludes:

> It is plain that such a religion as Christianity, which has for its object the worship of the Divine self-revealed in history, the Logos incarnate in time and space—which seeks and finds God self-given, in and through the littleness of the manger, and the shamefulness of the cross—is closely bound up with a sacramental interpretation of life.[4]

The service of worship and education and celebration at South Church is aimed at trying to recover a "sacramental interpretation of life." This intention has little to do with the technical ecclesiastical debates as to whether there are seven sacraments, or two sacraments, or none, in the Christian life. The intention is related to a much more general belief that, in Underhill's words, "the Supernatural draws near to man in and through the natural."

Communion, Consecration, and Sacrament

But how does the Supernatural come to us? How do people "seek and find the Eternal in the temporal"? How is it that the presence of Christ can be experienced in and through the whole of creation? How does the church, composed of finite human beings, actually go about consecrating significant events, objects, or relationships so that these may become vehicles for an encounter with the holy?

These questions are important for the entire three-part Sunday morning program. They are particularly important for the climactic celebration period, which includes a time designed to consecrate experiences in the church and the world. How the congregation attempts that consecration is crucial.

Yet these questions are also enormously difficult. In a fundamental sense human beings are unable to consecrate anything. Consecration involves waiting upon the Holy Spirit, who alone can reveal the presence of Christ. We cannot force the hand of the Holy Spirit. We can, however, create a climate of expectancy within which the church may be most likely to experience Christ's presence when and as it is revealed to us. Waiting upon the Holy Spirit need not be done in a vacuum.

The church knows something about the specific experience of consecration from the service of Holy Communion. The consecration of bread and wine in the Lord's Supper can provide a model for the consecration experience in celebration.

We may isolate five components in the consecration of the Eucharistic elements. First is the use of ordinary materials from secular life. The bread and the wine are not created out of special holy ingredients, but out of the same flour and grapes that are used for supermarket bread and grape juice and wine. In the same way the consecration experience of act three of the two-hour program may begin with a variety of common objects or events from the secular world in which we live.

A second component in the Communion consecration of bread and wine is the recalling by the church of the biblical narrative of the Last Supper. That narrative in the context of the life, death, and resurrection of Jesus Christ provides the basic setting within which the community of faith gathers today to experience Christ's presence. Similarly, the broader celebration act may include the attempt to relate significant areas of our contemporary life in the church and the world to the total story of the people of God in the Bible. As we do so, our life takes on new depth as a part of the continuing story of God at work in human history.

Thirdly, there is the Communion prayer for the Holy Spirit to consecrate the elements brought forward. And prayer is a central dimension of celebration, too. The prayers of act three may take a variety of forms: extemporaneous prayers, litanies, prayers set to music, silent prayer with an opportunity for people to pray out loud during that silence if they feel led to do so. Intercessory prayer is often a highlight of the consecration experience. Central to these prayers, whatever their form, is the recognition that it is God and not we ourselves who deepens faith and that we must open ourselves to him for that deepening.

The Lord's Supper contains a fourth component: an acting out of the breaking of bread, the pouring of wine, the sharing of both with the congregation. The variety of ways in which these actions are implemented in different denominations is ample testimony to the diversity of celebration patterns which are appropriate for different cultures or ages or theological points of view. Yet throughout this variety one sees the common thread of significant actions done in the atmosphere of worship which involve some or all of the congregation present.

A similar component can be found in the action of celebration. The congregation is invited to participate in a variety of actions. But instead of limiting these actions to the breaking of bread or the passing of the cup, the possibilities may include singing, laughing, weeping, dancing, processing, embracing, working, protesting, playing, eating, talking, rejoicing—as the Spirit moves. Some or all of the people who are present may respond to the invitation by entering into the activity of the moment.

There is a fifth component to the Communion meal, namely, the opportunity for the congregation to participate through faith. It is difficult, if not impossible, to try to demonstrate Christ's presence in a celebration of the Eucharist to an individual who is skeptical, apathetic, hostile. Rather, the Lord's presence is mediated through the Communion service to the faith of those who gather.

Likewise, the congregation may participate in the celebration experience through faith. No one can prove that Christ is present in the church's celebrating to the person who comes to act three with the attitude "I dare you to make me believe this has anything to do with the life of faith." But those who come to celebration in the expectation that the Holy Spirit will be there to meet them are often able to come away from that act with the belief that their expectations have been met. One man, for example, commented with obvious feeling after celebration at South Church one Sunday, "The Spirit was really here today." His testimony reminds us that our celebrating in faith can be fulfilled in Christ.

The Interaction of Communion and Celebration

The parallels between the celebration period and the Lord's Supper are numerous. We have already noted that the model order for act three which is printed in the South Church bulletin every week is borrowed from the Communion service. One may also take note of a common ecclesiastical usage of the verb *to celebrate* in conjunction with the Maundy Thursday meal: the church celebrates Communion.

Celebration may be described as a general pattern of worship, and the Lord's Supper as one particular form of that larger pattern. I believe that our life in the community of faith is impoverished if the Eucharist becomes by design or default the only significant celebration we participate in together. And our life is poorer still if a congregation's "celebration" of Holy Communion is so dry and dull and rigid that the experience is a travesty of the verb *to celebrate*.

One final dimension of the three-part Sunday morning program at South Church, therefore, is the hope of an ongoing process of creative interaction between that program and Holy Communion. The alternating rhythm of the Communion service on the first Sunday of the month and the three-part service on the other Sundays provides the opportunity for cross-fertilization between these services.

As the church moves from month to month, each service has a carry-over effect on the other. The Communion pattern helps to keep celebration from getting out of bounds and stimulates its growth in a faithful and responsible way. But celebration in return becomes an opportunity for the church to learn the richness and variety of moods which are appropriate to the presence of Christ in the Lord's Supper.

Too often the wider church seems to have been so paralyzed by the fear of being sacrilegious in Holy Communion that its members have not found the freedom to "rejoice in the Lord always." Perhaps that paralysis comes from reading too much into Paul's warning in First Corinthians, "Whoever, therefore, eats the bread or drinks the cup of the Lord in an unworthy manner will be guilty of profaning the body and blood of the Lord."

We can agree that a congregation of today should avoid the selfish individualism of the first-century church of Corinth, as well as any worship activity which would bring dishonor to Christ's name. But there is no reason to agree that such an avoidance must lock people into the lifeless ritual which Communion has become in so many parishes. Dignity and joy are not mutually exclusive.

The spirit of the celebration period at South Church is gradually making its way into the congregation's attitude toward the Lord's Supper. The ideas of celebration as congregational worship, as play, and as outreach have important implications for the particular celebration of the Eucharist.

Instead of understanding Holy Communion as a drama to be acted out by a few leaders for the rest of the people, we are coming to see that special service as a corporate drama to be celebrated by the whole congregation. As J. G. Davies puts it, "The renewed understanding of the corporate nature both of the Church and of worship has tended to issue in the emphasis that the celebrant at the eucharist is the congregation and that the function of the priest or minister is not to celebrate on behalf of or apart from the faithful but to preside."[5]

The Lord's Supper can be enriched, too, by a deeper feeling for the spirit of play. This spirit is not the same as irreverence. We quoted ideas earlier from the book *Using Biblical Simulations* which are as relevant to Communion as they are to the broader experience of celebration: "Faith is a play of the imagination. . . . The past is an open possibility to be regained by fantasy and imagination as well as hard research. Celebration and storytelling are how we recover who we are and where we are going."[6] Is not the Eucharistic fellowship with Christ an experience which beckons us to participate through faith as a "play of the imagination"?

The outreach dimension to Holy Communion is also significant. The Christ whose presence we celebrate around the Lord's Table is Lord not only of the church but of the whole world. As we gather to reenact that ancient meal of bread and wine, we come to find the strength to reach out to the corners of the world in the love of Christ Jesus.

A study group in South Church recently spent some time discussing the hypothetical question "What would you do today if you knew that Christ was going to return to the earth tomorrow?" One person responded that she would spend the rest of the day on her knees in prayer for forgiveness. Another commented that he would try to clear up all his debts and obligations. A third suggested cleaning the house.

But as the discussion developed, a different kind of response began to take shape. If Christ were to return tomorrow, shouldn't we spend the rest of today preparing a joyous celebration to welcome him? To this thought one participant added, "And I would want to make sure that a couple of people I know were invited to the party, people who I believe especially ought to have the chance to meet him."

Does not that study group discussion say something important about the richness of moods and responses which are appropriate to the presence of Christ in Communion? Praying for forgiveness, clearing up debts, cleaning up our possessions, and above all planning a party and inviting those from outside who need to be there—are not all of these actions also relevant to our preparation for the Lord's Supper?

Many in this parish remember vividly the Communion service in December of 1971 when we celebrated the unanimous adoption of a new constitution and bylaws after a year of church-wide reevaluation. During that service we read the story of God's saving acts in Christ; this portion of the Eucharistic Liturgy is sometimes called the "anamnesis," a transliteration from the Greek word for "remembrance" used in 1 Corinthians 11:24. Instead of limiting our remembering to those biblical acts, however, we opened the service to a corporate remembering of significant acts in the life of this congregation.

Coming after a time of polarization and turmoil this informal sharing of parish memories was both a healing and joyful experience. We laughed and cried together in the middle of Holy Communion. The broken body of Christ was all too real from our experiences in the preceding months. But long-standing memories of new life within the church coupled with the mood of unity and hope in the unanimous action of that night gave to the service an overflowing joy. Out of that Communion came the feeling and the longing for continuing experiences of celebration which would build on the bread and the wine but which could also move out beyond them.

Biblical Sacrifices and Offerings

The Lord's Supper itself grows out of a biblical background. A brief sketch of this background gives additional perspective to the relationship between Communion and the three-part program, and particularly between Communion and the climactic celebration act of that program. Such a sketch may also point the way to some of the biblical resources which can inform the church's celebrations today.

Possibly of most significance in the Old Testament is the elaborate system of sacrifices and offerings. One thinks, for example, of such passages as

> You shall seek the place which the Lord your God will choose out of all your tribes to put his name and make his habitation there; thither you shall go, and thither you shall bring your burnt offerings and your sacrifices, your tithes and the offering that you present, your votive offerings, your freewill offerings, and the firstlings of your herd and of your flock; and there you shall eat before the Lord your God, and you shall rejoice, you and your households, in all that you undertake, in which the Lord your God has blessed you. (Deuteronomy 12:5-7)

The people of ancient Israel took it for granted that eating and drinking a variety of foods was appropriate in the sanctuary. In the above passage, these people were commanded to find the holiest of all holy places and there bring a series of offerings: animals to be killed and roasted, grain and oil to be mixed in cakes, etc.

There were a number of reasons, such as simple thanksgiving, behind such offerings. One of those reasons was the belief that a meal eaten in the presence of God was a means of deepening one's relationship with the Lord. Just as the sharing of a meal with a friend may strengthen the friendship, so too the sharing of a meal in the Lord's presence may strengthen the ties which bind a person to him.

Some of the great Old Testament prophets, to be sure, spoke out strongly against sacrifices and offerings. Amos, for example, proclaimed:

> I hate, I despise your feasts,
>   and I take no delight in your solemn assemblies.
> Even though you offer me your burnt offerings
>   and cereal offerings,
>   I will not accept them,
> and the peace offerings of your fatted beasts
>   I will not look upon.
> Take away from me the noise of your songs;
>   to the melody of your harps I will not listen.

> But let justice roll down like waters,
> and righteousness like an everflowing stream. (5:21-24)

But these prophets were not protesting the whole system of offerings. Rather, they were against abuses of that system.

> Contrary to a widespread impression that there was a fundamental antithesis on this subject between the religion of the law and that of the prophets, the truth is that the latter were not against sacrifice per se, but simply against the abuse of it; and, as a matter of fact, Isaiah (1:15) inveighed equally against hypocritical prayer. Their protest was directed primarily against the attribution to sacrifice of properties and virtues which in fact it did not, and could not, possess; especially against the view that it expressed of itself the spiritual bond between worshiper and God, that God could thereby be persuaded or compelled, and that a man could be spiritually shriven by being ritually cleansed. Nowhere, however, in all the prophetic literature of the OT, is there any denial of the premise that, within its prescribed limits, sacrifice was indeed an effective religious vehicle; the advance beyond this assumption is entirely postbiblical.[7]

Sacrifices and offerings, in other words, were an accepted means of deepening the life of faith in the Old Testament. But when these offerings became the only responsibility of the religious person, then there was trouble. God's will encompassed the whole of a person's life, seven days a week. No sacrifice could be a substitute for a concern for justice and righteousness.

The New Testament Letter to the Hebrews understands the sacrificial system of the old covenant to be fulfilled in the perfect offering, once for all, of Christ on the Cross: "But when Christ had offered for all time a single sacrifice for sins, he sat down at the right hand of God, then to wait until his enemies should be made a stool for his feet. For by a single offering he has perfected for all time those who are sanctified" (Hebrews 10:12-14).

The ancient Israelites had abused the sacrificial system at times by believing that they could make themselves holy through eating and drinking in God's presence. The Letter to the

Hebrews claims that that temptation is removed in Christ. It is the death and resurrection of the Lord Jesus which alone makes human beings holy in the sight of God.

The New Testament, however, continues the older belief that there can be positive religious value in a sanctuary meal. Eating and drinking in the presence of God are ways by which people can open themselves to receive the consecrating Spirit which Christ offers to them. Food and drink do not compel God to do anything; such would violate God's absolute freedom and sovereignty. But food and drink can help to make human beings receptive to the gift of God's Spirit which he has promised to send.

The pages of the New Testament contain references to a variety of meals, including, but hardly limited to, the Communion meal—meals which deepen the faith of those who participate. Joachim Jeremias writes about the background for the "founding meal" of the Last Supper:

> In reality, the "founding meal" is only one link in a long chain of meals which Jesus shared with his followers and which they continued after Easter. These gatherings at table, which provoked such scandal because Jesus excluded no-one from them, even open sinners, and which thus expressed the heart of his message, were types of the feast to come in the time of salvation (Mark 2:18-20).[8]

The long chain of meals here includes the feeding of the five thousand in Matthew 14:13-21, a meal of bread and fish. It would also include the Easter meals of bread on the Emmaus Road (Luke 24:13-35), of broiled fish in Jerusalem (Luke 24:36-43), and the vaguely dated breakfast of bread and fish with the disciples by the Sea of Tiberias (John 21:1-14).

The meals of the early church were not limited to a repetition of the Last Supper, either:

> And they devoted themselves to the apostles' teaching and fellowship, to the breaking of bread and the prayers. . . . And day by day, attending the temple together and breaking bread in their homes, they partook of food with glad and generous hearts, praising God

> and having favor with all the people. And the Lord added to their number day by day those who were being saved. (Acts 2:42, 46-47)

One may also note the brief and unexplained reference to "love feasts" in the Letter of Jude (the twelfth verse).

Communion as the preeminent celebration of the New Testament community of faith draws much of its meaning from the rich history of sacrifices and offerings and meals throughout the Bible. But other celebrations can and do draw meaning from that same rich history. There is ample biblical precedent for the use by South Church of a variety of foodstuffs on the Lord's Table in our celebration service.

The whole world was shocked and saddened by the death and destruction in Honduras following Hurricane Fifi in September of 1974. Part of that tragedy was the loss of an overwhelming portion of the country's banana crop. An urgent plea was made for food, for money, for relief supplies. The hurricane's damage was brought before South Church as a concern during act three one Sunday.

One woman brought in a basket of bananas and placed them on the Lord's Table. After giving a brief description of the disaster, she offered to pass the bananas around to the congregation. Each person was to break off a piece of the fruit and eat it as a symbolic identification with the Honduran people. Then we were invited to replace the bananas we had eaten with money to be sent for disaster relief.

The symbolism was powerfully reminiscent of Holy Communion. Instead of breaking and sharing bread, we broke and shared bananas. The experience was not intended as a substitute for the Eucharist, but rather as an extension of it. As we lifted up symbolically the presence of the broken body of Christ in Honduran suffering, we were called to respond with compassion to people in need.

In line with prophetic criticism, however, one must be careful to proclaim that the eating of bananas and the giving of money in church does not satisfy our obligation as children of

God to the hungry people of the world. That celebration may have deepened our faith and our sensitivity to a particular tragedy. But act three, or the whole two-hour program, cannot become a replacement for the kinds of actions throughout the week to which the prophet Micah referred so long ago:

> He has showed you, O man, what is good;
> and what does the Lord require of you
> but to do justice, and to love kindness,
> and to walk humbly with your God? (Micah 6:8)

General Biblical Consecrations

The experience of consecration in the Bible goes beyond sacrifices and offerings and sacramental meals. And bread and wine, or food and drink in general, are far from being the only objects which serve as vehicles for the deepening of faith. If the consecration time in the South Church three-part program is an attempt to find the faith meaning in significant events, objects, and relationships from the whole of life, one may also find the roots of that larger effort in the biblical narrative.

An important dimension to the Old Testament is the search for the faith meaning in such critical *events* as the exodus from Egypt, the Assyrian defeat of Israel, the Babylonian conquest of Judah, the rebuilding of Jerusalem. It was largely the task of the prophets to articulate what God was doing in the midst of this history to fulfill his purposes.

The New Testament sees important faith meaning in the events of healing described throughout the Gospels; God's healing Spirit breaks into the plane of human history in and through the life of Christ. Jesus' cleansing of the temple (Luke 19:45-46), too, is an action designed to consecrate that building as a "house of prayer." And the washing of the disciples' feet (John 13:1-11) enables them to have a part in their Lord and encourages them to follow his example and serve others.

Old Testament consecrations involve a variety of *objects* as well as events. Amos looks at a plumb line (chapter 7) or a basket of summer fruit (chapter 8) and sees these as symbols of

God's impending judgment. Jeremiah watches a potter reshape a spoiled clay vessel, and the incident helps him to understand God's call for repentance (chapter 18). And Isaiah uses the symbol of a vineyard that yields wild grapes to set forth the reasons why God's patience is at an end with his disobedient people (chapter 5).

The record of the new covenant, too, is filled with objects which become important symbols of faith. Undoubtedly the chief of these is the Cross, an instrument of torture and death, which becomes the basic symbol of God's self-giving love. Jesus' death is the means whereby the Cross is consecrated.

One also comes across a number of relatively common objects which are used by Jesus to illustrate the content of his teaching: an unshrunk patch of cloth on an old garment; new wine and old wineskins; a lamp, a bushel, and a stand; a grain of mustard seed; a coin with a likeness of Caesar. The list includes lilies of the field, salt, leaven, treasure hidden in a field, a pearl of great value, and a camel and the eye of a needle.

Significant personal *relationships* in the Old Testament also become the means for the interpretation of faith. The relationship between Abraham and Isaac reveals the meaning of loyalty to God, particularly in the father's willingness even to sacrifice his son (Genesis 22). The Genesis story of Joseph and his brothers opens the door to an understanding of forgiveness (especially in chapter 50). And the prophet Hosea comes to a deeper feeling for God's covenant relationship with his people through a marriage to Gomer, an adulteress; that marriage serves as a window through which Hosea can see the anguish in God's love for an unfaithful nation.

Again, the relationship between Jesus and the twelve disciples becomes the foundation and the paradigm for the New Testament church. And Jesus' parables often build on personal relationships to illustrate the gospel message: the prodigal son (Luke 15:11-32), the good Samaritan (Luke 10:29-37), the Pharisee and the tax collector (Luke 18:9-14), the unforgiving servant (Matthew 18:23-35), the widow and the unjust judge (Luke 18:1-8).

This is only a sampling of the rich biblical record of people finding sacramental meaning in events and objects and relationships. A study of the full record reveals fertile soil in which modern celebrations of the community of faith may sink their roots and grow. When one adds the possibility of worship and education experiences integrated with those celebrations, the opportunities for growth in faith are magnified.

Children, Celebration, and Communion

Our discussion in this chapter of the Communion background for the two-hour service of worship, education, and celebration has emphasized the parallels between the Lord's Supper and the third act of that service. The interaction of Communion and celebration, however, raises one particular issue which deserves special treatment: namely, the question of the participation of children.

The South Church experience with the three-part Sunday morning program has confirmed the value of involving children in as much of that program as possible. Even the three-, four-, and five-year-olds make a special effort to join the rest of the congregation when it is time for act three. The inclusion of children does create discipline problems at times, but the reaction of most people may be summed up in the affirmative comment of one adult:

> Even though there may be occasional restlessness (though surprisingly little, I think), I like the presence of the children in worship and celebration—I get a sense of "church family" which I've not had before. I have liked the opportunity of working with children of mixed ages in two of the education classes. I would guess this would have meaning for the kids, too.

If children are welcome in all three acts of the three-part service, what happens to them when the congregation celebrates Holy Communion? In some denominations a child is not invited to receive the Sacrament until he or she has been confirmed; and confirmation classes may not take place until high school.

After considerable discussion on the part of the Boards of Deacons and Education in this Middletown parish, the decision was made "to invite children of our congregation to participate regularly in the Service of Communion, including the taking of the elements." No one, obviously, would be forced to accept the invitation; such acceptance was left to the wisdom and guidance of the parents of each parish child in consultation with the children themselves.

This decision in effect separated the two events of confirmation and first Communion. A child could be welcomed into the fellowship of the Lord's Table several years before being confirmed. As the Communion order of worship puts it, "We welcome to this table all who have been baptized in Christ, who desire peace with their neighbor, and who seek the mercy of God."

A family could also decide that an individual boy or girl was not ready to share responsibly in the Lord's Supper and guide that child to wait for a while. At confirmation, everyone would be welcomed to share in Holy Communion, regardless of whether he or she had done so earlier. The service of Confirmation would be the point at which a young person could first make the choice, independently of family guidance, to receive the Communion meal.

In essence, this congregation found it difficult to understand how we could invite children to celebrate the presence of Christ in act three on one Sunday and not invite them to celebrate his presence in the Eucharist on the next. If children were really a part of the church family, as we believe, then they ought to be fully involved in the climactic event of that family's life: the Lord's Supper. The interaction of Communion and celebration, coupled with the inclusion of children in the latter, led to the desire to include them in the former as well.

Opening the Lord's Supper to children, however, does not mean abandoning the importance of understanding that sacrament. It does mean a recognition that different age groups comprehend things at different levels. And a child, we believe, can understand enough of the significance of Holy Communion to enter into that celebration responsibly and to grow through continued participation.

If a five-year-old child were to ask her parents, "Where do babies come from?" the child would probably not expect or comprehend a biological treatise on the intricacies of the human reproductive system. A simple answer might well suffice: "They grow inside mommies." In a similar way, a five-year-old who asks his parents what Communion is all about need hardly be given a theological treatise on the mystery of the divine presence in finite space and time; a better answer might be the simple statement "God loves us." There will be time and reason as children grow older to expand on the simplicity of both answers.

The Protestant emphasis on rational understanding of the Lord's Supper prior to participation may need to be balanced with other emphases. The place to begin with many children today may not be in attempting to counter an absence of intellectual comprehension about Communion, but rather in trying to overcome a sense of alienation from the fellowship of the Lord's Table. It may be more important for the child to feel that he or she belongs to the community of people who celebrate Holy Communion than for that child to try to understand exactly what happens in that special service.

Many adults are unable to claim a comprehension of the Lord's Supper. No matter how young or how old a person is, no matter how much education that person has had, there is always room for growth in understanding of the mystery of the presence of Christ in Holy Communion. As long as the individual starts out on the right track with a general understanding of what is happening appropriate to that person's age, is there any reason why we cannot expect him or her to mature in understanding through the regular experience of sharing in the Sacrament?

It is worth remembering that some branches of Christianity treat the question of children's participation in the Eucharist with approval. One thinks of the Eastern Orthodox custom in which "infants are still baptized and confirmed and, except among the Chaldeans and the Maronites, communicated at the one service." There is also the Roman Catholic custom, prevalent since the late medieval period, "to confer confirmation as soon as convenient after the seventh birthday, while allowing children to communicate previously."[9]

Children are also important participants in the Jewish Passover Seder, a service of worship which is probably related to the Last Supper (which occurred at the season of Passover, if not on Passover itself). The youngest child present at the Seder plays a crucial role by asking the Four Questions about its meaning:

> Why does this night differ from all other nights? For on all other nights we eat either leavened or unleavened bread; why on this night only unleavened bread?
> On all other nights we eat all kinds of herbs; why on this night only bitter herbs?
> On all other nights we need not dip our herbs even once; why on this night must we dip them twice?
> On all other nights we eat either sitting up or reclining; why on this night do we all recline?[10]

The value of children's participation in Communion became clear to South Church, not through theological arguments over Communion and confirmation, nor through the practices of other religious communities. That value was demonstrated in the middle of an unplanned organizational oversight.

The Lord's Supper one year was to be celebrated on a Palm Sunday. With an unexpectedly large Holy Week congregation, we ran out of grape juice in the middle of the service. The deacons who were passing the elements to the people in the pews discovered that they had empty trays while two dozen persons were still to be served.

The minister tried to improvise a solution to the problem by asking all those without grape juice to raise their hands and all those with full cups to seek out a person in need and share. The solution seemed to work well, and the whole congregation was able to receive the cup. But when the deacons finally came back down the aisle to the front of the church, they suddenly remembered that they themselves were without grape juice—as was the minister, who is usually served last.

It happened that the children's choir was sitting in the front pew that particular morning, having sung an anthem earlier in the service. Some of the children noticed the deacons and the minister empty-handed around the communion table, and, since they were the closest, these children came to the rescue. Several walked up to the front of the sanctuary and sat next to the deacons in order to share the grape juice they had been given.

For the rest of that Communion service, the children and the deacons sat side by side on the special pews reserved for those who assist the minister in the administration of the Sacrament. The expression on the faces of those children—and of those deacons—was deeply moving for the whole congregation. The children in their actions had obviously understood something essential in the Lord's Supper.

Once South Church had made the decision to invite children to participate in the Communion meal, it was possible to support that decision through the Christian education program of the parish. Several courses in the second act of the three-part Sunday morning service have been aimed at the meaning of the Lord's Supper. And some of these classes have been specifically planned for the younger members of the church family.

One class in September of 1972 was planned for children in grades one through three. The first sessions were largely verbal—simple discussions on Communion as a means of sharing in God's love. On the final Sunday of the month the class came to church early to help mix and knead a batch of dough, and to eat breakfast together. The teen-age co-teacher had worked out a special recipe for what might be called "one bread in three acts": dough which would rise during the worship act, bake during the education act, and be ready for eating in celebration! Some of the bread was kept and frozen to be used for Communion the next Sunday, with the children in that class helping the deacons to serve it to the whole congregation.

A Final Word: The Risk of Presumption

The discussion on the Communion background for the three-part Sunday morning service requires a final reflection. I recently found myself talking with a clergyman about the South Church program and its relationship to the Lord's Supper. His first reaction to the intended relationship was negative.

Communion, as he saw it, was so sacred, so awesome, so unique, that it should be left in a class by itself. To try to create a service of celebration on the model of the Lord's Supper seemed to him to be presumptuous. An expanded or extended Eucharist could well have the effect of "pulling down" Communion from its rightful high and sacred position to a level where it could lose its power.

The criticism is worth listening to, since it represents a real risk in the three-part program. I believe, however, that the South Church experience to date contradicts that fear. Without very much being said about it, it is Communion which has exerted the influence on the celebration period by gradually "pulling it up" to a level of increasingly significant worship.

But there is a sense of inevitable presumption, nonetheless, in attempting to create a Sunday morning program on the foundation of the Lord's Supper. What right does one Connecticut congregation have to put its relatively meager creative efforts in the same liturgical arena with the vast, centuries-long wealth of theological elaboration on Holy Communion?

We may well have no such right. But the recognition of

presumption leads me to the fundamental affirmation that the three-part service of worship, education, and celebration is itself a human offering in need of consecration. At best it is one vehicle through which God in his mercy may choose to meet us. In actual experience the service may reflect far more of the broken body of Christ than of the new life he has promised.

We offer that service for whatever consecration God may choose to make of it in the lives of other churches and in the deepening life of our own congregation. We offer the possibilities in such a service along with those ancient words which point to the hope that these possibilities might be fulfilled: "Amen. Come, Lord Jesus!" (Revelation 22:20).

Epilogue

In a recent conversation with a friend who is a psychiatrist, I was describing the South Church service of worship, education, and celebration. He listened with particular interest. At one point he commented:

> That's fascinating! What you are doing is using the same progression in church that I've seen in a number of non-church gatherings: an opening formal presentation for the whole group, followed by a splitting up into small groups for discussions or other activities, and a closing session in which the small groups rejoin each other to share highlights of their experience with the large group.

His insight was valid, though no one had pointed it out in quite that way before. There is a similarity between the three-part Sunday morning program and that relatively familiar process used in many meetings across our society. Each step in the program builds on what has gone on earlier. And there is a progresssion of increasing challenge from the first part through to the last.

We began to expand on the insight. The worship act at South Church requires a low level of personal involvement with a large group of people; there is little need to interact with those around you in a formal service. In the education act, a member of the congregation is faced with the challenge of a higher level of personal involvement; but the challenge is made easier by the small number of people in any given class. By the time of the final celebration period, the individual may have been able to gather the courage to confront the climactic challenge—a high level of personal involvement with a large group of people.

Formal worship places few demands on the worshiper. The open-endedness of celebration, however, is far more difficult and far more demanding for most people. The education act in between serves as a bridge, an intermediate experience leading from act one to act three. An individual who chooses to become involved in the full two-hour program is led, therefore, through a process that gradually frees him or her to be able to enter into the experience of celebrating.

That conversation with my friend was helpful. And it was pleasing to know of an important secular parallel for the three-part service, one which might well enrich the biblical and religious background we had already developed. Here, in effect, was an argument of support and reinforcement arriving on the scene long after the church had made the original decision to adopt the two-hour program.

The 1972 decision to start out on a new course was made, to be sure, after a long process of thought and discussion. The decision grew out of the experience of success and failure, joy and suffering, enthusiasm and discouragement. From the perspective of hindsight, however, the choice looks more and more like a leap of faith. We understood very little of what we were doing at the time. Our decision was largely an illustration of the policy "Leap now—learn why later."

What has been so rewarding ever since 1972 is the fulfillment of that policy: the more we have learned why, the more we rejoice at having been led to make the leap in the first place. Perhaps such fulfillment is the meaning of grace. The secular insight of my psychiatrist friend is not the only argument of support and reinforcement that we have discovered after the fact of beginning the three-part service. A major share of the theory presented in this book has been developed and refined in the light of our actual experience of worship, education, and celebration.

There are problems, of course. A new look for Sunday morning can lead to an over-focus on what the church does on that one day at the expense of a concern for the Christian life in the rest of the week. A service of worship, education, and celebration can bring new diversity of church life, but it cannot do everything; one must be careful to guard against an overexpectation of what is possible in two hours.

The congregation can create the problems of in-groups and out-groups if people are insensitive. Those who choose to stay for all three acts can convey the feeling that others who leave after formal worship are somehow "out of it." We have had to emphasize again and again that people are welcome for the total program, but that all are free to begin wherever they are most comfortable and to stay for as long or as short a time as they want. We hope, in time, that many will decide to participate in the full two hours, but that decision must be made by the individual person without a sense of guilt if the response should be more limited.

Other areas in the life of South Church are acquainted with the same problems of most parishes. The three-part Sunday morning program is no cure-all for financial headaches, for attendance drops, for difficulties in finding enough qualified leaders for everything the congregation wants to have done. Day-to-day parish life in Middletown still needs an abundant willingness to exercise the biblical commandment to forgive sins.

In spite of difficulties such as these, however, we believe there is value in the vision of an integrated Sunday morning program of worship, education, and celebration. As one person put it, "If there weren't, we would have given up long ago." The two-hour program is not a superficial effort to "jazz up" a

Sunday school or a church service. It is rather an attempt to integrate the fellowship of the church family. Integrating a program is related to integrating people.

Most church congregations today, one expects, are filled with a diversity of persons. What is important is to find an overall unity which affirms that diversity. St. Paul stated the idea long ago in words which are quoted in the South Church bylaws for the Board of Deacons: "Now there are varieties of gifts, but the same Spirit; and there are varieties of service, but the same Lord; and there are varieties of working, but it is the same God who inspires them all in every one. To each is given the manifestation of the Spirit for the common good" (1 Corinthians 12:4-7).

So often, too, our own personal life of faith is compartmentalized into unrelated segments: our worship (by ourselves or in church) has little connection with our learning in the field of religion, and the kind of experience which has been described here as celebration is isolated or ignored in still another corner. Integrating the life of the parish may set an example which can aid us in integrating our religious life as individual persons within that parish.

The vision and the reality of the three-part Sunday morning service may well be summed up in a letter of evaluation written by the president of South Church several months after the service was initiated. His comments are a good summary for this book:

> This responds to requests for comments on our Sunday morning worship experience at South Church. I refer to the whole two hours, for even though they are divided into three parts, for me at least it is a total worship experience.
>
> Although there may be some bugs in our experiment I think it has become a most satisfying and exciting experience, and should be kept just about as it is. No longer is "worship" divided from "religious education." Though we may separate for a period of time the opportunity to rejoin in the celebration period seems to and indeed serves to pull together the service into a full "worship experience." One church member has told me that the full worship service—

worship, education, celebration—and the atmosphere of South Church fellowship gives him a sense of peace and understanding and excitement such as he obtains in no other way. . . .

The transition of South Church from a church where the adults gathered each Sunday from eleven to twelve o'clock to sit stolidly in their pews in order to be "ministered to"—to a church where members of all ages sit together, where people can feel free if they wish to take part vocally in a corporate prayer, where occasional applause and laughter can be heard, and where in a worshipful atmosphere we minister with each other—this is a strange and wonderful transition. Especially when one considers that many of the same people are involved. I think this transition and our feeling of Christian fellowship has been strengthened immeasurably by our worship experience. It is my hope that we can continue it.

Notes

Chapter 1

1. Robert W. Lynn and Elliott Wright, *The Big Little School* (New York: Harper & Row, 1971), p. 97.

Chapter 2

1. Evelyn Underhill, *Worship* (Torchbooks; New York: Harper & Brothers [1936], 1957), p. 3.
2. *Ibid.*, pp. 14, 34-35.
3. *Ibid.*, pp. 298, 299, 235.
4. *Ibid.*, pp. 27-28.
5. *Ibid.*, pp. 110-11, including n. 1 on p. 111.

Chapter 3

1. Quoted in *The Bible and the Public Schools,* ed. with commentary by Arthur Frommer (New York: Affiliated Publishers, 1963), p. 78.

Chapter 4

1. As quoted in *Simple Gifts,* vol. 1, ed. by Gabe Huck (Washington: The Liturgical Conference, 1974). See the article "Without a Word," by Donald Wiseman, p. 46.
2. Donald E. Miller, Graydon F. Snyder, Robert W. Neff, *Using Biblical Simulations* (Valley Forge, Pa.: Judson Press, 1973), pp. 10-11.
3. *Ibid.*, p. 11.
4. *Ibid.*
5. Harvey Cox, *The Feast of Fools* (Cambridge, Mass.: Harvard University Press, 1969), p. 13.
6. *Ibid.*, p. 75.

Chapter 5

1. Evelyn Underhill, *Worship,* p. 42.
2. *Ibid.*
3. *Ibid.,* pp. 44-45.
4. *Ibid.,* p. 46.
5. J. G. Davies, *A Select Liturgical Lexicon,* Ecumenical Studies in Worship Number 14 (Richmond: John Knox Press, 1965), p. 48.
6. Donald E. Miller et *al., Using Biblical Simulations,* pp. 10, 11.
7. *The Interpreter's Dictionary of the Bible,* R-Z (Nashville: Abingdon Press, 1962); see article "Sacrifices and Offerings, OT," by T. H. Gaster, p. 157.
8. Joachim Jeremias, *New Testament Theology* (New York: Charles Scribner's Sons, 1971), pp. 289-90.
9. J. G. Davies, *Select Liturgical Lexicon,* pp. 22, 58.
10. As quoted in *The Passover Haggadah,* based on the commentaries of E. D. Goldschmidt, ed. by Nahum N. Glatzer. Trans. of the Haggadah text by Jacob Sloan. Rev. ed. (New York: Schocken Books [1953], 1969), p. 21.